CALLAGHAN
A Life

This abridged edition is selected by the New Statesman from the standard edition of this work. The standard edition, published in September 1997, is available from bookshops or directly from the Oxford University Press warehouse.

Special Offer
Save £2 from the retail price of £25

Readers of the New Statesman are entitled to a £2.00 discount per book from the retail price of £25 plus free postage for orders up to and including three copies. The offer is ONLY available by either phoning the OUP 24-hour hotline on 01536 454 534, or faxing your order to 01536 454 518, or sending your order to:

CWO, Customer Services Department
Oxford University Press Distribution Service
Saxon Way West
Corby, Northants
NN18 9ES

In order to receive your discount you MUST cite the following code AT001
This offer ends at 12 noon on 31 October 1997

Please note: the special offer is only available directly from the Oxford University Press warehouse.

CALLAGHAN
A Life

By KENNETH O. MORGAN

OXFORD UNIVERSITY PRESS

1997

Oxford University Press, Great Clarendon Street, Oxford OX2 6DP

Oxford New York

Athens Auckland Bangkok Bogota Bombay
Buenos Aires Calcutta Cape Town Dar es Salaam
Delhi Florence Hong Kong Istanbul Karachi
Kuala Lumpur Madras Madrid Melbourne
Mexico City Nairobi Paris Singapore
Taipei Tokyo Toronto Warsaw

and associated companies in
Berlin Ibadan

Oxford is a trade mark of Oxford University Press

Special abridged edition for the New Statesman

Published in the United States
by Oxford University Press Inc., New York

© Kenneth O. Morgan 1997

British Library Cataloguing in Publication Data
Data available

Library of Congress Cataloging in Publication Data
Morgan , Kenneth O.
Callaghan: a life / Kenneth O. Morgan.
p. cm.
Includes bibliographical references (p.).
1. Callaghan, James, 1912– . 2. Prime ministers—Great Britain—
Biography. 3. Great Britain—Politics and government—1945–
I. Title.
DA591.C34M67 1997 941.085'092—dc21 97–19750
ISBN 0-19-820216-4

1 3 5 7 9 10 8 6 4 2

Typeset by Hope Services (Abingdon) Ltd.
Printed in Great Britain by
Biddles Ltd., Guildford & King's Lynn

Preface

THE career of Lord Callaghan is inseparable from British history in the second half of the twentieth century. In many ways he is one of its representative figures. He has played a part in British public life for well over sixty years. He became a union official in 1933 and he is an active peer in 1997. His longevity in politics exceeds that of Lloyd George and rivals that of Gladstone or Churchill. Not even they managed to hold all the major offices of prime minister, foreign secretary, chancellor of the Exchequer, and home secretary which Lord Callaghan uniquely has done. No one else better embodies the rise and decline of the social democratic consensus that largely shaped British history for the three decades after the end of the war in 1945. His fall from power in 1979 was commonly taken as marking the end of an era. Many commentators then saw him as Labour's last prime minister, a prophecy which events in May 1997 were to demolish. Lord Callaghan is a symbol of our present as well as our recent past, New Labour as well as Old. He links the age of Clem Attlee and that of Tony Blair.

The art and craft of biography are subtle and contentious. The relationships of author and subject have been extensively, often passionately, discussed. In my own case, this book is an official biography in the sense that I have had unhindered access to Lord Callaghan's personal archive of 55 boxes and to Lord Callaghan himself. But it remains a totally independent work of history. He has not revised my judgements. Nor indeed, since he has already written a work of autobiography, did he wish to. I do not feel in any way compromised by my own relationship with my subject. I met him intermittently in earlier years, notably when I chaired an election meeting at which he spoke in Swansea West back in 1959. But I had little contact with him over subsequent decades until we met again in early 1989 after my appointment as a vice-chancellor in the University of Wales. I was an academic observer of his career but never in any way a participant in the events described in this book. I do not feel inhibited by the fact that Lord Callaghan is still alive. I hope and believe that I have written in the same spirit of frankness and independence as if he were a figure in the past. In any event, a biography such as David Douglas's fine study of William the Conqueror, or almost any book by Arthur Schlesinger, Jr., reminds us that bias towards one's subject is not confined to the living.

There is, obviously, one colossal gain in writing the biography of a living person, namely the ability to talk freely with my subject on anything I choose. In writing earlier books of mine, how I would have loved to talk to Keir Hardie or David Lloyd George. In the case of Keir Hardie, who died twenty years before I was born (despite his firm belief in spiritualism and a recorded account of a conversation with him at a socialist seance on 26 July 1945), I did at least talk to the late Fenner Brockway. He was able to give me many insights into Hardie (whom he first met in 1906) that I simply could not have obtained elsewhere. The personality of Lloyd George was much illuminated for me by conversations with two of his children, his nephew, and some of his grandchildren. In the case of this contemporary leader, Lord Callaghan, alive, well, and mentally in full vigour during the eight years in which I was writing this book, I needed no such intermediaries.

Biography is a kaleidoscopic art form. In this book, I was concerned to go beyond merely describing the career of one important figure, and to revert in part to an earlier literary tradition. The great majority of my previous books have not been biographies. I have tried here to write something akin to the more traditional 'life and times', to set Lord Callaghan's career against the context of Britain's domestic and international history from the 1930s to the 1990s, and locate it within the distinctive evolution, tradition, and mythology of the British Labour movement. I have greatly benefited from the recent flowering of contemporary history in this country. It is the public man, the national and world figure, who has been my main concern. I do not think that a psycho-biography of Lord Callaghan would be of any great interest, even assuming I was professionally competent to produce one. On the other hand, Lytton Strachey has long taught us that the public and the private are virtually impossible to disentangle. Lord Callaghan's ancestry, personal characteristics, and style of life, his views on religion and culture, on public and personal morality, on family, friendship, and foreign lands are an essential part of trying to explain his career and draw out the fullest implications of his role in the making of the modern world.

My main thanks must be to Lord Callaghan himself for asking me to write a book which has given me such extraordinary enjoyment and stim-

ulation over the past eight years, as well as to Lady Callaghan for much
personal kindness and hospitality. In addition to subjecting himself to, I
imagine, dozens of meetings (informal open-ended conversations, not
tape-recorded interviews) with invariable frankness, courtesy, and good
humour, Lord Callaghan also gave me free range over his archive of fifty-
five boxes. They form a very substantial collection which spans his life in
all its aspects from his career as a trade union official in the early 1930s
onwards. It contains a wealth of correspondence, manuscript notes and
jottings, transcripts, reports, *aides-mémoires*, and sections of diaries. The
Callaghan Papers have gone to the Bodleian Library in Oxford, where
they will lie alongside those of Attlee, Macmillan, and Wilson amongst
other post-war political figures, and I hope that they will shortly be made
available to other scholars. During the writing of this book, I was much
indebted to successive keepers of the House of Lords Record Office, Mr
H. C. Cobb and Mr D. J. Johnson and their staff of the House of Lords
Record Office who looked after the main archive from 1990, and latterly to
Mrs Mary Clapinson of the Bodleian and Dr Angela Raspin of the LSE for
their help in arranging the transfer of material to the Bodleian.

Beyond this, I have incurred an immense range of obligations over the
past eight years. I am much indebted for formal interviews with Lord
Allen of Abbeydale, the late Lord Bancroft, Dr Nigel Bowles, Lord Brooks
of Tremorfa, Sir Julian Bullard, Sir Alec Cairncross, Michael Callaghan,
Baroness Castle, Sir Brian Cubbon, Dr Jack Cunningham MP, Sir
Geoffrey de Deney, Lord Donoughue of Ashton, Gwyneth Evans, David
Faulkner, Michael Foot, Lord Gladwin of Clee, Geoffrey Goodman, Roy
Hattersley, Lord Healey, the late Lord Houghton of Sowerby, Lord Hunt
of Tanworth, Lady Jay of Paddington, the late Lord Jay of Battersea, Peter
Jay, Lord Jenkins of Hillhead, Jack Jones, Dr Henry Kissinger, His
Excellency Lee Kuan Yew, Professor Ian Little, Sir Thomas McCaffrey,
Tom McNally, Lord Merlyn-Rees of Cilfynydd, Alun Michael MP, Lord
Murray of Epping Forest, Lord Rodgers of Quarrybank, His Excellency
Helmut Schmidt, Roger Stott MP, Sir Kenneth Stowe, and Alan Watkins.
I have also benefited from information, often extensive, kindly provided
by Donald Anderson MP, Kenneth Baker, Lord Blake, Albert Booth,
Ken Bovington, Lord Bullock, Natasha Burkhardt, Tony Christopher,
Professor Brian Clarkson, Lord Cledwyn of Penrhos, Edmund Dell, Dr
N. H. Dimsdale, Mrs Marjorie Durbin, Emrys Evans, Dr Ewen Green,
Harry Green, Kenneth Harris, Professor Peter Hennessy, Sir Reginald
Hibbert, Lord Hooson, Lord Hunt of Llanfairwaterdine, Lady Jay of
Battersea, Rt. Hon. Neil Kinnock, Sir Montague Levine, Robert

Maclennan MP, Professor David Marquand, Leslie Monckton, Mrs Margaret Park (UW Swansea), W. G. A. Raggett, Gerald Rees (Bank of Wales), John Sadden, Dr Jean Seaton, Peter Shore MP, Olive Tanton, Professor Charles Webster, Baroness Williams of Crosby, and Jessie Worrall.

I am very grateful to the following libraries and archive centres for permission to quote from papers in their possession: the Public Record Office; the Bodleian Library, Oxford (Attlee, George-Brown, Greenwood, Boyd of Merton); Rhodes House Library, Oxford (Creech Jones, Welensky); the National Library of Wales (Cledwyn, Donnelly, Griffiths, Tonypandy); British Library of Political and Economic Science (Crosland, Dalton); Modern Records Centre, University of Warwick (Cousins, CBI, IRSF); Clive Brooke (Inland Revenue Staff Federation papers); Lyndon Baines Johnson Library, Austin (Johnson, Fowler); Gerald R. Ford Library (Ford); Jimmy Carter Library (Carter). I am also indebted to Mr John Cousins for access to the Cousins Papers, to Lady George-Brown for access to the George-Brown Papers, and to Lord Cledwyn and Lord Tonypandy for access to their papers. Professor Ian Little kindly let me use his papers on the economics seminars of the early 1960s. My old friend Sir Alec Cairncross, himself an eighth wonder of the world, allowed me to use his MS diary as well as his important study of economic policy in the 1960s, prior to publication. Lord Tonypandy, Rhodri Morgan MP, Baroness Williams, Peter Shore MP, Dr Jack Cunningham MP, David Lipsey, and Sir Goronwy Daniel allowed me to print extracts from letters to which they own the copyright. I can only apologize if, through mischance or inadvertence, I have failed to trace or acknowledge any other authors.

I am also most grateful for help regarding source material to Lord Donoughue, Christine Woodland (Modern Records Centre, Warwick), John Graham Jones (National Library of Wales), Geoffrey Goodman and Tony Christopher (Lord Houghton papers), Stephen Bird (Labour Party archives), Harry Middleton and Michael Parrish (Lyndon Baines Johnson Library), Martin Elzy (Jimmy Carter Library), Leesa Tobin and Nancy Mirshat (Gerald R. Ford Library), Robert Morgan (BBC Today programme), Kirsty White (BBC archive), Hywel Francis (UW Swansea), Nick Crowson and Virginia Preston (Institute of Contemporary British History), and the library of the Athenaeum. Like so many historians I am deep in the debt of the Public Record Office and its good-natured staff over the years.

I have also appreciated the opportunity to try out my ideas on the matters discussed in this book in seminars or public lectures at a variety of institutions. I am therefore most grateful to invitations successively from the University of Malaya (Kuala Lumpur); the National University of Singapore; the Aberystwyth Rotary Club; the Stubbs Society, Oxford; the University of Wales, Swansea; the University of East Anglia; the University of Tübingen (Baden-Württemberg); the University of Wales, Aberystwyth, History Society; the graduate research seminar at St John's College, Oxford; the Universities of the Witwatersrand, Cape Town, and Western Cape, South Africa, and the University of Sheffield.

Many learned colleagues and friends have generously given their time in commenting upon all or part of this book. Professor Vernon Bogdanor of Brasenose College, Oxford, read the entire text and offered a host of stimulating suggestions or corrections; I am deeply in his debt, as also to the anonymous reader for Oxford University Press. I also benefited from the learning of Dr John Darwin of Nuffield College and Dr Nick Owen of Queen's on colonial policy, Dr Nicholas Dimsdale of Queen's on economic policy, Professor Richard Rose of Strathclyde on the premiership, Dr John Rowett of Brasenose on modern political history, Professor Roger Hood of All Souls and my late wife Jane on penal policy, and Dr Nigel Bowles of St Anne's on recent politics, quite apart from his own close association with Lord Callaghan since 1979. I have, as always, benefited from conversation with my friends Dr Alastair Parker of Queen's and Dr Denis Balsom, warden of Gregynog, as well as with Tim Bale of Sheffield University. Obviously, blemishes and errors that remain are my responsibility and mine alone. I would like to mention also the endlessly cheerful help of Gina Page, Lord Callaghan's secretary, and his driver, Alan Currie, and of my two wonderful staff at the university in Aberystwyth, my personal assistant Nan Thomas, and my secretary Beryl Jones. Indeed, Aberystwyth as a whole was remarkably generous in allowing its vice-chancellor the opportunity to retain a foothold in the historical world. My literary agent Bruce Hunter, a mentor and good friend over a quarter of a century, has always been a fount of encouragement. Tony Morris of OUP has once again been the most unstuffy of editors, and my old friend Ivon Asquith a firm rock of reassurance. I am also indebted to the advice of Kim Scott-Walwyn, and the calm efficiency of Mick Belson, Amy Turner, and Juliet New.

To my children, David and Katherine, my debt is beyond words. They have materially helped this book (not least by explaining to a grossly nontechnical father how word-processors work!), they have been eternally cheerful, and they have shown immense reserves of courage when the most important person in our lives, my beloved Jane, was so cruelly taken from us. They have shown me and each other love and endless loyalty. At a time when such a thing appeared somewhat elusive, they have given me a reason to live. Diolch o galon!

K.O.M.

Long Hanborough
8 May 1997

22

PRIME MINISTERIAL STYLE

'IF action and inaction seem equally valid, then act.' This perhaps unlikely precept, announced in a Hubert Humphrey memorial lecture on 'The Political Leader' at the University of Minnesota in 1982, embodied James Callaghan's philosophy of the prime ministerial role.[1] He was sometimes dismissed by commentators as a cautious fixer rather than one to take charge of events, condemned by critics as various as the diplomat Nicholas Henderson and the Tory politician Norman Tebbitt as hesitant and indecisive. Tony Blair once accused his predecessor of failing to take decisions; business went 'through umpteen committees which meant things never got done at all'.[2] But Callaghan did believe in a doctrine of leadership and sought to put it into effect as Prime Minister. In his Hubert Humphrey lecture he made a distinction between different types of leadership, somewhat as Max Weber had done in his analysis of 'charismatic leadership' long before. Callaghan spoke of 'visionary' leaders (such as Gandhi), 'inspirational' leaders (Churchill, Roosevelt, and 'my own fellow countryman [sic] David Lloyd George'), and 'consensus' leaders, amongst whom he classified himself. But while he emphasized the need to take a broad global view of a leader's role and stressed the reciprocal relationship between leader and led, he felt it essential for a political leader to seize the initiative and provide an active and engaged sense of direction, from both the strategic and moral point of view. The fact that his three years of premiership were constrained by the absence of a Commons majority and the need to conciliate various small minority groupings did not change his ultimate approach.

This was the kind of role he undertook from the outset as Prime Minister. He acted with a decisiveness and vigour which not only belied his 64 years, but surprised many observers of his previous career. He attended to every detail, including that of his own physical well-being: as he had done during his time as Foreign Secretary, he gave up alcohol entirely, and took care to conserve his energy through regular short cat-naps during the day, a practice dating from his time in the navy. He worked in an intense and concentrated fashion all his own, often taking important papers home with him, perhaps to read in his study or even in bed, in a pri-vate, almost introverted way. His style was to hear all the arguments and not rush in recklessly to reach an early conclusion. Without doubt, he made a more enduring and positive mark as premier than he had ever done at the Treasury, Home Office, or Foreign Office. He is an unusual case of a leading British twentieth-century politician who left No. 10 not discred-ited as premiers before him from Asquith to Wilson had been, but with his public reputation significantly enhanced. Yet he did so not as a remote and domineering personality in the mould of Margaret Thatcher, but as the generally trusted leader of a team.

Callaghan's standing as Prime Minister, of course, was derived largely from the way he conducted himself in the supreme office. But it was, at least initially, based on the simple fact that he was not Harold Wilson. His predecessor, while widely admired as a wily tactician of legendary capacity for survival who had actually won four elections out of five, had fallen in public esteem by the time he left office. Civil servants found him increas-ingly unimpressive as a leader, forgetful and erratic in carrying out deci-sions. One cause appeared to be his consumption of brandy which made him less effective after lunch. Callaghan, by contrast, imposed a firm grip on the agencies of government from the very start. The decline in Wilson's reputation was to continue long after he retired, probably to an excessive degree. But, judging from some of the obituaries, it may be ques-tioned whether the appearance of distinguished biographies in the early 1990s produced a significant process of rehabilitation.

By April 1976, Wilson was widely attacked not so much for policy fail-ures, or the substance of his regime, but rather for his style. To the general public, he seemed almost a paranoid figure, obsessed with 'leaks' and 'moles', engaged in witch-hunts against the press or the BBC or unnamed adversaries in MI5. His public standing had never really recovered since his unfortunate television broadcast to the nation immediately after deval-uation of the pound in November 1967 when he assured the voters that the pound in their pocket had not been devalued. He was never wholly cred-ible again. It was Wilson's equivalent of Stanley Baldwin's 'appalling frank-ness' speech about rearmament in the 1930s which led to Winston Churchill's celebrated index entry in his war memoirs, 'Baldwin, Stanley, puts party before country'. On a personal basis, Cabinet colleagues and civil service advisers almost universally felt that, while Wilson was personally a kindly and generous man of great talent, the devious way in which he ran his administration undermined a sense of trust. This was also widely believed by Commonwealth leaders such as Lee Kuan Yew.

Callaghan, by contrast, a bluff and far more direct figure, seemed in this key respect to be a great improvement. Voters could identify with his prejudices, hesitations, and very English pragmatism. He was a severe taskmaster and could be fierce towards civil servants, especially when they appeared sloppy or ill-prepared. On one occasion in Karachi he reacted furiously when the British ambassador to Pakistan seemed to him inadequately briefed, and walked out of a dinner in the embassy in disgust. It was also thought that he could be uneasy at first with new appointments: some felt that Bryan Cartledge suffered a little in this respect. Even so, there was hardly one minister or civil servant amongst those who served under both premiers who did not feel a breath of fresh air and a cleaning out of Augean stables when Jim Callaghan entered No. 10. There was a more genuine sense of collective participation and collaborative endeavour on the part of the administration as a whole, and far more sense of loyalty. In particular, there was nothing resembling the Wilson 'kitchen cabinet' which had met with widespread disapproval, especially with the publication of volumes of memoirs by Marcia Williams, Lady Falkender, by Wilson's press secretary Joe Haines, and others. This had been a growing impediment to Cabinet cohesion. The personal entourage of Wilson was felt to be acting in at best a quasi-constitutional way, promoting its own prime ministerial agenda and instilling a kind of bunker mentality in Wilson himself. The penumbral role of George Wigg, as a kind of personal bloodhound for the Prime Minister sniffing out plots and leaks, had not been conducive to a happy atmosphere either.

Callaghan's premiership had nothing remotely like this. He had not got on badly with members of the Wilson entourage. Indeed in the case of Marcia Falkender he had a good working relationship. It had been Callaghan who first enlisted her to work for the Labour Party after he met her at a student political meeting at the end of the 1950s. (As noted earlier, when asked what her particular merits were, he replied good-humouredly, and not unreasonably perhaps, that she had 'beautiful blue eyes'.) There was some complaint about the kind of machine politician the new Prime Minister had tended to attract: Gregor MacKenzie and Roland Moyle were sometimes a target of criticism in this respect, especially from ministerial victims like Gerry Fowler. But his own group of personal advisers, notably Tom McNally and Tom McCaffrey who followed Joe Haines as press secretary, played a more orthodox and visible role than their predecessors and aroused no such antagonism. Comparatively speaking, a new era of open government seemed to begin on 6 April 1976 and so it was to remain. It should be added that Harold Wilson, who gradually diverted his energies to writing volumes of political reminiscences and a series of television programmes on previous prime ministers, made no difficulties of any kind for his successor. Unlike Lady Thatcher after 1990 he never claimed to be any kind of back-seat driver. Three weeks after Callaghan had taken office, Wilson wrote warmly to him accepting an invitation to Sunday lunch with the Callaghans. 'I am, naturally, watching and approving the course of events and the attacks made on the problems. A good start.'³

Callaghan inherited the formal structure of government that had operated under Harold Wilson in 1974–6, and indeed basically under Edward Heath in the 1970–4 Conservative administration. The essential governmental machinery consisted of the Cabinet Office, under its secretary Sir John Hunt, and the prime minister's private office, under the direction of Sir Kenneth Stowe. Between the two, so Bernard Donoughue believed, there was a dualism, almost a kind of discreet rivalry, which gave Whitehall observers (and connoisseurs of the TV series *Yes Minister*) some private amusement.⁴

The Cabinet Office, since its foundation under Sir Maurice Hankey and Thomas Jones when Lloyd George first became premier in December 1916, had a broad set function of servicing the Cabinet and its attendant committees. But it also had from its early years an agenda which included policy-making, although this varied according to the outlook and personality of the Secretary. Sir John Hunt, who had already served under Edward Heath and Harold Wilson since 1973, was among the more vigorous exponents of this tradition. He had some years earlier chaired a working party on rail transport during Barbara Castle's time at the Transport Ministry and continued to show an interest in policy-making. A firm Roman Catholic whose wife was the sister of Cardinal Basil Hume, he had a viewpoint of his own. His style as Cabinet Secretary appeared different from that of his subtle predecessor Burke Trend. He was a manager not a mandarin, more forceful and with more evident ambition to be active executively, especially on the economic side. Callaghan encouraged him in this. One early instance was the way in which Hunt suggested the agendas for the Prime Minister's various meetings with departmental ministers. Thus on 15 July 1976 his brief for Callaghan's projected meeting with Peter Shore listed such potentially controversial topics as housing finance (including a possible move away from a general subsidy), housing's share of public expenditure, the role of building societies, possible governmental devolution in England, the inner cities, and local government finance: he noted that the Layfield Committee had recommended a 'local income tax'. He observed that Shore 'does not always give the impression of being a happy man at the DOE and that his strength lay in intellectual argument rather than executive decision-making in a department of 70,000 people'.[5] He also offered views on Cabinet-making. In July 1976 he offered the view that if Merlyn Rees were to be moved to the Home Office in succession to Roy Jenkins, the Northern Ireland Office might conceivably go to a peer.[6]

The Cabinet Secretary naturally took a keen interest in the machinery of government. Early in 1977 Hunt was proposing to Callaghan a scheme agreed between himself and Sir Douglas Allen for dividing up the Treasury into a Ministry of Finance, and a bureau of the budget covering public expenditure and manpower. The Chancellor would focus on taxation, customs and excise, the mint, and national savings.[7] Callaghan appeared to have some sympathy with this idea and might well have tried to implement something like it had he won the 1979 election, with Denis Healey being moved to the Foreign Office. But, perhaps because it was too reminiscent of former troubles with George Brown and the DEA, nothing resulted. On a different tack, Hunt offered Callaghan in 1977 his candid views on the effectiveness of the various Cabinet committee chairmen. Healey was 'outstanding' and rarely lost the thread of an argument. Merlyn Rees was at best average and did not give a clear enough lead. David Owen was brisk but could be impatient. Shirley Williams was good but could be overrun when the going got rough. Michael Foot relied unduly on his brief. Altogether, Hunt's view of his role was more than merely functional. Tony Benn claimed to see in his operations a potential danger, especially in the way that he appeared to use Berrill and the CPRS as an arm of central government. In practice, Hunt's effective influence upon policy-making was episodic, although Donoughue noted approvingly that he acted as a 'very positive' chairman of a Cabinet committee on unemployment in 1978.[8]

Hunt's main role was to service and support the Prime Minister, although of course he served ministers in general. At various times, but particularly in 1977, he and Callaghan actually contemplated the idea of a prime minister's department to provide the fullest range of information and authority for No. 10. This was a proposal considered at times by Wilson, Heath, and Mrs Thatcher as well. However, Callaghan concluded, surely correctly, that it was unnecessary since 'all the levers of power' were fully at his disposal in any case.[9] The Policy Unit almost fulfilled this role. More generally the idea might revive old memories of Lloyd George's Garden Suburb of ill repute in 1918–22, and thereby make the Prime Minister appear unduly presidential. Hunt approved of the collective way in which Callaghan ran his government and got on well with him personally. He was much impressed by the Prime Minister's ability to focus on selected key issues. He did not, however, operate in Downing Street itself and was, therefore, somewhat distanced from the epicentre of decision-making in contrast to the private office under Stowe who operated in the very next room to the Prime Minister. For this, and perhaps other reasons, Hunt for all his energy and air of self-confidence was not felt by some observers to exude quite the same authority under Callaghan's premiership that he had done under Wilson in 1974–6, or Robert Armstrong was to do under Mrs Thatcher. On the other hand, the calm way in which he handled security and other matters helped to restore equilibrium in the central administration after the near-paranoia of the Wilson years.

The private office consisted of civil servants on secondment who ensured that the Prime Minister was properly briefed and generally sorted out the details of his day-to-day activities. Under Callaghan the somewhat overpowering personality of Robert Armstrong gave way to the more unassuming and congenial figure of Kenneth Stowe. Somewhat unusually, his previous experience had mainly been in the DHSS rather than in the Cabinet Office. He and the Prime Minister struck up from the first an excellent and enduring relationship; Callaghan particularly appreciated his sensitive awareness of the political context in which policy decisions were taken. It was Stowe who proposed on 28 April 1976 that Callaghan might involve himself more directly in relations with his ministers than Harold Wilson had done. The implication was that the former Prime Minister had been unduly detached and remote.[11] Callaghan, he suggested, might ask his ministers for short reports on departmental matters, as a way of informing himself (and, no doubt, keeping ministers on their toes). He might also suggest individual initiatives in policy 'in the context of regular and thorough consultations with them about their stewardship'. Following Stowe's initiative, the first such meeting was held with Fred Mulley, Secretary for Education, on 21 May, with meetings with Tony Benn (Energy), Bruce Millan (Scotland), Peter Shore (Environment), and David Ennals (Health and Social Security) to follow shortly. Thereafter, Stowe's quiet and judicious presence was a major factor in almost all aspects of government policy, domestic and overseas, from the attempts to frame a wages policy to relations with European colleagues such as

Schmidt and Giscard d'Estaing. He was also a crucial figure in the party negotiations that led to the Lib–Lab pact in March 1977. His strong relationship with the Prime Minister was founded on a high level of trust and mutual regard. It is a testimony to the impartiality of the British civil service tradition that Stowe was apparently to enjoy an equally cordial relationship with Mrs Thatcher.[12]

The other members of the private office were of equally high calibre. They included secretaries seconded from the Treasury. Of these Nigel Wicks was regarded by the Prime Minister as exceptionally able. He had the additional merit that he was never overawed by Treasury mandarins, since from 1968 to 1975 he had been one himself, following long experience of the petroleum industry. He also went far beyond the Treasury brief on occasion, for instance in giving examples of the populist style of Mrs Thatcher's campaigning rhetoric.[13] Wicks was succeeded in 1978 by another Treasury man, Tim Lankester. There were also two former ambassadors, not of course members of the home civil service, to advise on foreign affairs. Patrick Wright, a career diplomat and authority on the Middle East, had been Callaghan's private secretary at the Foreign Office and was in due time to become head of the diplomatic service. His successor, Bryan Cartledge, a future ambassador to Moscow, was an adviser on eastern Europe in particular, who was to accompany the Prime Minister on several overseas visits.[14] He developed a very high regard for Callaghan's diplomatic skills and sense of statesmanship. He admired his expertise in east–west relations and his idealistic commitment to the third world. His one serious error, so Cartledge believed, and one from which Kenneth Stowe might have dissuaded him, was the appointment of his son-in-law Peter Jay as ambassador to the United States. At a more routine level, David Holt kept the Prime Minister's diary, and Philip Wood assisted with the preparations for question time in the House.

Beneath this formal level of interacting Cabinet and private offices, there was a second level of advisers. This consisted of two institutions, one more important and more intimate with the Prime Minister than the other. The more tangential body was the Central Policy Review Staff, popularly known as the Think Tank. It had been set up by Edward Heath under the chairmanship of Lord Rothschild. Under Callaghan it was headed by Kenneth Berrill, formerly chief economic adviser to the Treasury, with Dick Ross as his deputy (Gordon Downey replacing Ross in 1978).[15] Its personnel included a very able younger woman member, Tessa Blackstone, whose particular specialism at that time was overseas development, although she was also to be involved in education.

Callaghan defined the CPRS's role as fourfold—'to think the unthinkable, to give a global picture through assessments in the round, to fulfil particular assignments in problem areas, and to inject a new angle in agreed interdepartmental papers'.[16] The last two were held to be of most importance. Its role, therefore, was broadly strategic, even visionary. How this worked in practice was another matter, and Callaghan tended to use the CPRS less than Heath had done in a wide-ranging capacity. The CPRS, however, could be very useful to the Prime Minister. He could use it to point out weakness in ministerial papers and to alert him to problems in advance. The CPRS was also involved on occasion in high policy, as when there was a complex discussion on long-haul aircraft in 1977 and some pressure on British Airways to develop a relationship with British Aerospace rather than with Boeing. Tony Benn's 'alternative economic strategy' during the IMF crisis in late 1976 was also grist for the Think Tank's mill. Tessa Blackstone was used in the important role of following up the famous Ruskin speech on educational reform in October of that year.[17]

The CPRS, however, was detached and episodic in its impact on Callaghan's policy. By contrast, his Policy Unit was more ideological and constant in its involvement. One clear instance of the different roles of the two came in the summer of 1978 when the merger of the tax and benefit systems, as a result of the start of child benefits (which Callaghan had originally opposed when Barbara Castle put it forward), brought the theme of the 'family' into sharp political focus. This was a subject which naturally appealed to the Prime Minister himself. However, while the CPRS was engaged on a somewhat theoretical exercise in looking at family structure, gender relationships, and matters of that kind, the Policy Unit had the practical task of relating the theme of the family to aspects of government policy from education to vandalism and crime. It also encouraged the Prime Minister himself to pronounce on the topic. This he did with relish, notably in a widely reported speech to the General Assembly of the Church of Scotland (22 May 1978) in which he extolled the importance of 'a sound and sure family life'.[18]

Callaghan inherited the Policy Unit from Harold Wilson in 1974. It was perhaps the latter's most important constitutional innovation. The Unit's capacity to range over the whole spectrum of domestic policy, from exchange rates to Scottish and Welsh devolution, made it little short of a prime minister's department, his private fount of ideas. To a degree political scientists have yet fully to take on board, it marked a revolution in government. Its head, Thomas Cromwell to Callaghan's Henry VIII so to speak, was an ex-academic, with an interest in both financial and educational policy (and also in football), Dr Bernard Donoughue, formerly a politics lecturer at the London School of Economics. It was perhaps unusual for him to be retained in post by the succeeding prime minister. But Donoughue, in fact, was beginning to detach himself from Harold Wilson during the leadership contest in March–April 1976. It is significant that he was invited to attend the drinks party for Callaghan's triumphant campaign team after the contest was over.[19] Although he had no expectations of continuing in government, he played a strong and creative role for the remainder of Labour's term in office. He found Callaghan somewhat more formal than Wilson in their working relationship but, if anything, even more formidable in his intellectual power and executive decisiveness.[20] The fact that both he and Callaghan shared a working-class background and a pragmatic outlook on life made the bond between them closer still. Donoughue told Cledwyn Hughes in 23 July that 'he very much enjoys working for Callaghan and is much impressed by his style—thoughtful and relaxed'.[21] He enlisted a powerful and gifted team in his Unit, and they poured out advice and policy positions for the Prime Minister over the next three years. These started with Donoughue's own important memorandum on 'Themes and Initiatives' (PU 175) on 16 April 1976. This outlined the need for new policy initiatives from the Prime Minister on such issues as home ownership for council tenants, schools curricula, and voluntary social service, under the heading of 'Social Responsibility and Social Cohesion'.[22] In some ways, the Policy Unit under Bernard Donoughue anticipated the keynotes of Tony Blair's 'New Labour' philosophy of communal citizenship in the mid-1990s.

His team, many of its members being university teachers, was remarkably young and dynamic. They included, as full-time or part-time personnel, Andrew Graham, a 33-year-old Fellow in economics at Balliol, Oxford, who worked on macro-economic issues, especially incomes policy and balance of payments and energy policy; Richard Smethurst, a 35-year-old macro-economist who worked briefly on monetary policy, a Fellow of Worcester College, Oxford; David Gowland, a 27-year-old economist from the University of York; and Gavyn Davies, only 26, an exceptionally able statistician and econometrician, also from Balliol College, Oxford, for whom Callaghan had a particularly high regard and whom he encouraged to give advice on the whole range of economic policy options. This group, reminiscent of the Oxbridge group who had advised Callaghan in the Nuffield seminars when he was shadow Chancellor in the early 1960s, could deal confidently and on a basis of intellectual equality with the Treasury's advisers at any level. In addition, there were the 30-year-old

David Piachaud, a lecturer at the London School of Economics who specialized in social policy, health, and consumer affairs; Richard Graham, a manager from British Airways; Catherine Carmichael, a lecturer in social administration at Glasgow University; James Corr, from the World Bank, whose responsibilities, rather strangely, covered both trade union matters and Scottish devolution; Richard Kirwan from the Centre for Environmental Studies, a housing expert; and Elizabeth Arnott from the Transport House research staff. In 1977 they were joined on a full-time basis by David Lipsey, a 28-year-old Oxford graduate who had been special adviser to Tony Crosland for the past five years and whose remit covered, among other things, election strategy.[23]

There are several points of interest about these individuals. Among other things, they dispel the canard sometimes promoted that Callaghan was ill at ease with intellectuals or academics, especially those from an Oxford background. Evidence of his insecurity was sometimes cited. An Oxford-educated Labour member (said to be Bryan Gould) Callaghan allegedly turned down as a Minister for the Arts on the grounds that 'he makes me feel as if I had just come down from the trees'. Certainly he was often needlessly oversensitive to apparent slights or to being patronized. But it was pretentiousness not professionalism to which he objected. The personnel of his Policy Unit suggests both his high regard for specialist expertise, and the respect and loyalty that his advisers, mostly Oxford-trained from Bernard Donoughue down, felt in turn for him. After the uneasy atmosphere of the Wilson period of leadership, Callaghan's premiership seemed for many to enshrine, in a term applied to American politics, the rule of 'the best and the brightest'. On the other hand, some aides felt that it had been something of a weakness in his earlier periods in office, notably at the Treasury and the Home Office, that he had allowed himself to be surrounded only by mundane politicians like Gregor MacKenzie or Roland Moyle. The absence of powerful intellectual advisers then, they believed, had led to his being unduly swayed by his civil servants, in contrast to his marked confidence and stature as Prime Minister. Nevertheless, with advisers like Neild and Kaldor at the Treasury for instance, Callaghan had hardly lacked intellectually high-powered officials earlier in his career.

By the time Callaghan had become premier, the Policy Unit was established. Its relationship with the Cabinet Office and the central governmental committee apparatus was comfortably negotiated. On occasion its perceptions could come into conflict with those of the CPRS. Thus in December 1976–January 1977 there was a revealing argument between

Berrill and Donoughue about the Policy Unit's draft programme for National Recovery. Berrill felt this was too much addressed to the government's own supporters, and was too wide-ranging. It should focus on a few particular themes such as North Sea oil, industrial regeneration, and education. The Policy Unit, however, saw no difficulty in appealing mainly to Labour supporters. Gavyn Davies felt that the National Recovery programme's hopes for economic revival were perfectly justified, while Bernard Donoughue expressed surprise that the Think Tank was so devastatingly critical and negative.[24] On balance, it was the Policy Unit's more political stance that carried the day. In any case, differences of view like this were a part of constructive government rather than a sign of an innate structural conflict between the two bodies. Callaghan welcomed creative tension within the ranks of his advisers, even if he never followed Franklin Roosevelt's approach of encouraging antithetical viewpoints from ideologically opposed groups and then 'weaving the two together'. The New Deal was not an administrative paradigm for the British government. Nor was Callaghan-style creative tension a continuation of the Wilson approach of divide and rule.

The Policy Unit was an ideas machine of much potentiality. It was, for example, a frequent critic of the Treasury. It was under Callaghan that it came into its own. He used it with particular effect during the IMF crisis in November–December 1976 when it supplied much material designed to isolate Tony Benn and explode the credibility of his 'alternative economic strategy'.[25] This was satisfactorily achieved, although with some difficulty, for example in the light of Benn's subtle advocacy of the cause of import controls which was attractive to many not on the left.

Beyond this, Donoughue and his colleagues supplied a steady stream of papers on key issues, detailed and strategic. In June 1977, for instance, there were proposals on broad government economic strategy with an eye to the next general election.[26] At the same time, ways were suggested to deliver material benefits to Labour voters and neutralize the appeal of Mrs Thatcher ('Selsdon Woman').[27] In July 1977, attention was urged to reclaim the support of women voters for Labour.[28] In September there followed proposals for a £3 bn. reflation in 1978–9.[29] A year later, the Unit proposed a new range of initiatives with a view to a forthcoming election, notably the NHS (especially the hospital service), unemployment and technical change, law and order, and 'democratizing society', relating to such matters as industrial democracy, the running of schools, and a tenants' charter in housing. Callaghan responded very positively to all of them, especially the last, which he chose to redefine as 'citizens' rights, responsibilities and participation'.[30] In the course of the election campaign in April 1979 the Policy Unit was fertile with ideas for Labour to capture the political initiative and point out the inadequacies of Thatcherism.[31] Donoughue was encouraged by Callaghan to send in memoranda on all feasible topics, and felt that in general they landed on fertile ground. Only in the first three months of 1979, when the Prime Minister was tired and dispirited after the disappointments of the 'winter of discontent', was it felt that the Policy Unit was no longer able to influence his mind and outlook.

There was a final level of governmental machinery. This was the most intimate of all. It consisted of the Political Office and the press office, headed respectively by Callaghan's trusted aides Tom McNally and Tom McCaffrey. McNally had impressed Callaghan immensely both with his sensitive awareness of the balance of factors within the Labour Party and the trade union movement, and with his wide understanding of international issues, during the time that Callaghan was Foreign Secretary. With his master now in No. 10, McNally fulfilled all this role and much more besides, both as a liaison with the troublesome NEC and the unpredictable trade union movement, and as a generator of ideas on any topic that interested him, domestic or external.[32] On issues ranging from European monetary union or Rhodesia to the pact with the Liberal Party, McNally offered a stimulating stream of ideas, always tailored to the practical needs of leading the Labour Party as well as governing the country.

There appears not to have been any particular difficulty in the Political Office liaising with the Policy Unit or intruding into the more formal machinery of the civil service. McNally sought an early meeting with Sir Douglas Allen (head of the civil service), Kenneth Stowe, and Bernard Donoughue, to find a flexible formula through which the political advisers could participate in the planning of future programmes.[33] This proceeded satisfactorily, though McNally had to raise with Stowe on 21 September 1976 civil service objections to the appointment of David Hill, his long-standing adviser, as formal private adviser to Roy Hattersley who had just joined the Cabinet.[34] But these boundary difficulties were invariably resolved harmoniously and turf wars were almost non-existent. Callaghan had the highest regard for McNally's ability right down to the election campaign in 1979, by which time the latter had become Labour candidate for Stockport South. He for his part admired Callaghan's strategic judgement, his ability to absorb new, technical information on matters relating to economic or defence policy, and his general methods of running his administration. It was McNally who saw Callaghan at his most intimate, his period of high political finesse during the IMF crisis, his indecision over calling an election in August 1978 (when McNally himself was left in the dark like everyone else), and the final phase of near-despair during the winter of discontent. He also got used to Callaghan's routine in Downing Street (where he and Audrey lived, in contrast to Harold Wilson who had commuted from Lord North Street)—the early start, the short catnaps, the teetotal approach to hospitality, and the zest for foreign travel. As troubleshooter, lively ideas man, and friendly companion, McNally was unique.

In the closest touch with McNally was Tom McCaffrey, Callaghan's press officer as he had been at the Home and Foreign Offices. In contrast to his predecessor Joe Haines, McCaffrey kept a lower profile and concentrated on working on relations with journalists and the lobby generally.[35] Almost without exception he conducted his duties to Callaghan's total satisfaction, while the press liked him because he did not mislead them. A rare cause for complaint came at the sensitive moment of Peter Jay's nomination for the Washington embassy, when McCaffrey appeared to make disparaging noises about the snobbish demeanour of the present incumbent, Sir Peter Ramsbotham. Like McNally he saw Callaghan at close hand and much admired him, including on a human basis: one instance was when the British Prime Minister was called upon for marital advice by Pierre Trudeau, the premier of Canada, whose young wife was involved with a member of a rock group. Like McNally too, he remained unaware of Callaghan's decision about a possible autumn election in 1978 and found himself in some difficulty with journalists who had been briefed by others that an election was inevitable. McCaffrey and McNally invariably worked in unison and formed similar general views. One rare episode when their judgements did not coincide was over the press conference that followed Callaghan's return from the Guadeloupe summit in January 1979.[36] This event, with its resultant headlines of 'Crisis, what crisis?', was a sign of tired leadership and an administration heading for a fall. One intriguing episode was that Callaghan was advised by Geoffrey Goodman to take on a prominent and forceful pro-Labour journalist from Yorkshire as his press adviser. In fact, Hugh Cudlipp was to be chosen instead and it was Mrs Thatcher who enlisted the services of Bernard Ingham.[37]

Backed by this formidable range of advisers and administrative machinery, Callaghan handled his Cabinet with confidence but also consideration. He was well liked by them all. David Owen was to note his particularly sympathetic, human response when Owen's young son fell dangerously ill soon after he became Foreign Secretary.[38] Many difficult moments were defused by straightforwardness and good humour; the relationship with Tony Benn was far more amiable than might have been imagined, at least until the final months of trade union militancy and near anarchy. Callaghan had to give him stern warnings early on of the need to observe collective responsibility and had no patience with his minister's tortuous attempts to differentiate between speeches he made as a Cabinet minister and those he made as a member of the National Executive.[39] Callaghan emphasized that the general public took an integrated view of Tony Benn and regarded him as one and indivisible. Even though Benn contrived to the end to give the impression to his left-wing followers that he was both a member and an opponent of the Cabinet at the same time ('semi-detached' was the popular journalists' adjective for his posture), the Prime Minister kept him in line with more success than Wilson had been able to do.

Otherwise personal harmony and even loyalty prevailed. One Cabinet minister found the Prime Minister supportive when the tabloids tried to pursue him over an extramarital affair of potentially scandalous import; another, suspected of homosexual proclivities, was also left undisturbed. A close aide felt that Callaghan was immensely supportive to him while he was undergoing a particularly painful breakup of his marriage.[40] There were good precedents for this tolerance and compassion. It could even be said to reflect 'Victorian values' in contrast, say, to the stern puritanism of Clement Attlee. Even the virtuous Mr Gladstone, after all, had for long turned a blind eye to the liaison of Charles Stewart Parnell with Kitty O'Shea.

Callaghan felt in total command from the outset. On a personal basis, he felt secure living in No. 10, instead of being a non-resident as he had been at the Foreign Office. Audrey Callaghan found the house alarmingly large and the kitchen arrangements less convenient than on the farm. But as always she was an immense support for her husband. Cledwyn Hughes wrote in March 1977, 'I have always liked her; she is pleasant, even tempered, and a real help to Jim.'[41] No. 10 had the merit of being relatively close to Great Ormond Street children's hospital with which she was now most heavily and fruitfully involved as chairman of the Board of Governors. It was a crisis for the Prime Minister if any misfortune overtook his wife. He was deeply anxious when she had a minor car accident when leaving Downing Street in February 1977 after which hospital treatment was required. When he visited her there afterwards, he was falsely accused in the press of dodging an awkward Cabinet. In early 1978 she was mildly unwell and this again caused the prime minister some worry. But generally the family context was deeply reassuring. The children and grandchildren were frequent visitors. Michael Callaghan, now a senior manager in Ford Motors, found it fascinating to compare his business experience with the conduct of industrial policy as seen from Downing Street.[42]

On the political front, Callaghan felt relaxed and confident. After all, he had held all the key portfolios and had known other key departments either under Attlee or as Opposition spokesman. His background in this sense, ranging from the Dock Labour Scheme to the affairs of central Africa, was exceptionally well informed. He felt he knew the idiosyncrasies of every major department. In particular, he retained both respect for and suspicion of the Treasury, knowing how their refusal to consider the political context had brought difficulties for him during his time as Chancellor. His civil service aides, however, believed that he never showed the innate suspicion of the Treasury felt by Harold Wilson and such advisers as Joe Haines. In addition, as Governor of the Bank of England, Callaghan had the much more congenial figure of Gordon Richardson, instead of the imperious Lord Cromer whom he had considered a constant irritant during his own time at the Treasury. His deputy was an old friend, Kit McMahon, a member of the Nuffield group of advisers back in 1962–3. While Callaghan had particularly close friends in Merlyn Rees and Harold Lever, he did not play favourites in the Cabinet, and preferred a dialogue with colleagues as a whole rather than one-to-one mediation with individuals. He offered equal opportunity to younger ministers such as Shirley Williams, Roy Hattersley, and John Smith to participate in full in Cabinet deliberations. He usually chose not to give a view before asking for contributions to discussion in Cabinet, but summed up with both skill and fairness. As chairman he was lucid and concise, and he expected his ministers to be the same. Like other prime ministers from Attlee to Thatcher, he asked for Cabinet submissions to be brief.[43] On the other hand, like all experienced politicians, he could divert a discussion his way. Thus when William Rodgers wanted to introduce compulsory seatbelts, the Prime Minister managed to get a discussion on the issue delayed until just before lunch. He himself was opposed to compulsion on populist grounds. Rodgers's proposal nevertheless was supported by the majority, David Owen speaking vigorously in its favour. Callaghan then handed it over to the leader of the House, Michael Foot, who opposed compulsory seatbelts on libertarian grounds, and the chief whip, Michael Cocks, another opponent, and the proposal got no further.[44]

On balance, in major setpiece discussions, particularly during the IMF crisis but on many other issues including wages policy or the British nuclear deterrent, Callaghan's government was remarkable for its demonstration of the full potentialities of collective responsibility on the classic lines of Cabinet government. Richard Crossman's diagnosis that 'Prime Ministerial government' had become the norm, the view advanced in his famous introduction to the new edition of Bagehot's *The English Constitution*, was shown to be, at least in this instance, quite misconceived. Indeed Crossman had reluctantly come to disavow his own thesis after his own experience of being in Cabinet from 1964 and Harold Wilson's apparent lack of a sense of strategy thereafter. But, of course, as with all prime ministers from the Younger Pitt onwards, the style varied, as did the circumstances. Callaghan's broad-based Cabinet, with a tiny or no parliamentary majority, was to give way to Margaret Thatcher's virtual autocracy, based on landslide majorities, in which on occasion she appeared to dissociate herself from the decisions of her own Cabinet, as over the EMS. John Major, with whom Callaghan had a good relationship, reverted from 1990 to something more like the collective style of his Labour predecessor. After 1992, indeed, he came to emulate him not only in method but in his vanishing parliamentary majority.

Callaghan dominated his Cabinet more completely than Wilson did, at least in 1974–6, for all his alleged insecurity as a non-graduate from a humble social background. He was helped in this by sheer chance or misfortune. The removal of Roy Jenkins to take up the presidency of the European Commission in Brussels, followed soon after by the untimely death of Tony Crosland, meant that two of the major heavyweights of British public life were removed, and succeeded by younger and less illustrious ministers. The sacking of Barbara Castle at the outset had removed another possible source of alternative power. Tony Benn, by contrast, never enjoyed anything like the same stature within the Cabinet that he did amongst the left-wing activitists in the constituency parties and many of the trade unions.

The two key ministers, without doubt, were Michael Foot and Denis Healey. Foot, newly ensconced as leader of the House and effectively deputy prime minister, was essential to Callaghan as his link to the left, especially in the trade union movement. The Prime Minister would make a particular point of consulting Foot in private on all key issues well in advance to ensure that they were of like mind.[45] In the handling of wages policy and industrial relations generally, this was of central importance to the government's fortunes. Callaghan ensured that Foot attended all meetings and dinners with the TUC's 'Neddy Six'. He entrusted him with key negotiations in the framing of the Lib–Lab pact. He also encouraged him to participate in Cabinet discussions where Foot, a passionate tribune on the public platform, sometimes appeared unduly modest or reticent. In return, Foot, while never an intimate of the Prime Minister (he and Jill Foot never once visited him on the Sussex farm, for instance), was totally and unambiguously loyal. Bevan's disciple, he fought shoulder to shoulder with his ex-Gaitskellite colleague, right down to the final defeat over devolution in March 1979. His view was a decisive factor in dissuading Callaghan from holding a general election in the autumn of 1978.[46]

The other major figure was Denis Healey, the Chancellor of the Exchequer. The course of events ensured that economic problems would dominate the government's fortunes henceforth; from the summer of 1976 this meant that the Prime Minister himself was totally involved in economic policy-making, despite his initial wish to concentrate on foreign affairs. There were some who believed that the Prime Minister, rather than the Chancellor, was truly in charge of running the economy. Nevertheless, Callaghan and Healey, old colleagues though not exactly close friends, formed a powerful alliance together, and Callaghan backed up his Chancellor through thick and thin. There was a period at the height of the IMF crisis when it appeared that a major rift over policy was occurring, and there was some inaccurate journalists' talk of Healey being removed from the Treasury. There were further disagreements when Callaghan insisted that the Chancellor limit the concessions on public expenditure to be made as a condition in the letter of intent to be signed prior to receiving the massive loan from the IMF.[47]

But thereafter the two men were as one in coping with economic challenges, including the final, vain attempt to impose a pay norm of no more than 5 per cent upon the recalcitrant unions. They had a high regard for each other. Callaghan had great respect for Healey's intellectual powers (a view shared by Healey himself) and recognized that by 1976 his command over the Treasury was a strong one. In the event, Healey was to stay on as Chancellor for the full five years, perhaps two more than Callaghan himself felt was desirable for anyone. By 1978 Cledwyn Hughes felt strongly that Callaghan regarded Healey as his likely successor, or rather as his desired successor, as Wilson had felt about Callaghan himself in 1974–6.[48] Hughes gave Healey the good advice that he should spend more time in the Commons cultivating friends. For his part, Healey felt Callaghan to be a decisive, clear-headed, courageous leader,[49] whose political dexterity could cover up the consequences of his own occasional blunderbuss politics in handling friends and foes alike. In his memoirs he was to describe Callaghan as the best prime minister since Attlee.[50] Healey and Callaghan formed a powerful alliance, as indeed did Healey and Foot in their turn, particularly in negotiations with the trade unions. Had Labour won the 1979 election, Healey would have moved to the Foreign Office.

Callaghan encouraged his ministers to use their own initiative and to act as independent and trusted advisers. But that did not preclude him from trying to find policy areas in which he could pursue a line of his own, either as a stimulus or goad to ministers, or else as a forerunner of general Cabinet strategy. Tom McNally, Kenneth Stowe, and Bernard Donoughue and his Policy Unit colleagues were all active in suggesting areas where this kind of prime ministerial initiative could most effectively be exercised. Donoughue had taken the lead in Callaghan's first few days as premier, as has been noted. He proposed such themes as the sale of council housing and teaching standards in the schools as areas where Callaghan could assert himself. Tom McNally offered a not totally dissimilar list of priorities comprising the sale of council housing again, Northern Ireland (with an emphasis on social and economic progress), the social services, Scottish government, and education.[51] Callaghan responded to these with varying degrees of enthusiasm. Northern Ireland, for instance, was unfruitful territory, and the transition from Merlyn Rees to Roy Mason as Secretary for the province in September 1976 meant in practice an emphasis on hard-line law and order policies rather than an attempt to find a political consensus. In any case, with provisional Sinn Féin heavily involved in a campaign of murder and bombings, that was scarcely possible. There seemed to be no durable political settlement on the horizon. All Callaghan could hope for was to keep channels open as Oliver Wright had done for him in 1969–70 when British representative to the Stormont regime. Nor did Scottish government seem a promising area for a prime minister always cool on the possibility of Celtic devolution. On the sale of council houses, Callaghan recognized that here, like comprehensive education, was a traditional Labour shibboleth where public opinion, including working-class opinion, was changing. But he felt unable to promote a change of policy here and Labour's policy of maintaining a public housing stock remained intact. Labour publicists like Joe Haines were to lament, with some reason, that this failure left the way open to one of the more popular aspects of Thatcherism.

One particular theme, however, that he did make his own, and on which his personal authority was stamped, was education. In his ministerial meeting with Fred Mulley on 21 May Callaghan spelt out his long-standing concern with standards of teaching in the schools, the content of the curricula in different subjects, the promotion of science and technology, and the need for ensuring basic standards of literacy and numeracy amongst schoolchildren.[52] Earlier in the decade it was the political right which had taken up this issue. There had been 'Black Papers' from Baroness Cox and others since 1969, and proto-Thatcherite educational pressure groups that owed much to London experience, notably in the North London Polytechnic and the William Tyndale school. But Callaghan rightly felt that educational standards were, if anything, of even more concern to his own supporters since it was they above all whose children went to the maintained state schools. Now was the time for Labour to hit back. Although it caused much concern amongst officials in the Education Department, therefore, the Prime Minister began to assemble his thoughts for a major pronouncement on education. He enlisted the help of Bernard Donoughue of the Policy Unit, and later of Tessa Blackstone of the Think Tank, in its implementation. The outcome was the famous Ruskin College speech of 16 October 1976, much of which was written by Donoughue.[53] In the long term it inaugurated a 'great debate' on standards in public education which was still in full swing in the mid-1990s. It encouraged Labour to adopt a less doctrinaire approach towards state schools, and to consider aspects of high professional standards and quality controls. It was also perhaps the best example of the Prime Minister independently pursuing his own agenda and initiative, more openly than Macmillan or Wilson, more selectively than Heath or Thatcher. It was Jim Callaghan's version of prime ministerial government in action.

On this and other occasions, Callaghan was anxious to articulate his government's philosophy by means of an overarching theme. In the Ruskin speech it was public standards, related to social cohesion and responsibility by a citizenry in charge of its own destiny, aware both of its rights and of its duties and social obligations to others. On other occasions, it was the need for a more equal society on which Callaghan focused his attention, especially in speeches which concentrated on the reform of the social services, for instance in regard to child allowances or pension arrangements in promoting a fairer society.[54] At other times, it was more decentralized society which he emphasized, although this was not perhaps a theme embraced quite so enthusiastically. But certainly Callaghan was one of the more philosophical prime ministers, anxious to have it seen that his government stood for perceived values and that theory and practice went hand in hand. Honesty and integrity were particular themes of his speeches. By comparison with the manoeuvrings of the Wilson years, let alone the sleaze and scandal which gave rise to the Nolan Committee in

1994, his administration appeared to embody them. Callaghan made a strong impression when he appeared before that committee as the champion of higher standards of conducting public life, standards which his own government could reasonably be claimed to embody.

Sociological themes were also a part of the prime ministerial attempt to seize the political initiative by taking the moral high ground. The values of neighbourhood and particularly of the family were also themes which he emphasized and of which, by character and inclination, this singularly 'unpermissive' ex-Home Secretary seemed a most appropriate champion. His views, like those of many of his advisers (not to mention the vast majority of Labour voters), were in this area traditional and conventional. He was perhaps the first major politician to realize the wider political significance of merging the tax and benefit scheme, with the introduction of child benefit in 1978. His speeches now emphasized the 'family budget' as well as recognizing the power of the family, including especially the middle-class family, as a political and social pressure group. Enlisting a variety of Christian organizations in his support, he called for children to have 'a proper upbringing and a proper sense of values'. He urged parents 'to face up to their responsibility', for instance in ensuring decent day-care for their children when mothers went out to work. In his public pronouncements the silent majority seemed to find a clarion voice, while Mrs Thatcher, for the moment, seemed to be wrong-footed.

The other obvious theme of prime ministerial initiatives was that of law and order, one that came most naturally to the former spokesman for the Police Federation. He criticized the Labour Home Policy Committee in November 1977 for its comparative neglect of the problems of violence and vandalism, felt most acutely in working-class communities such as inner cities. In this he found an unexpected ally in the left-wing Liverpool member Eric Heffer. Back in September 1974 Callaghan had told the Cabinet, 'I am rather in favour of dealing with teenage hooliganism', to which Denis Healey gave a loud 'hear! hear!'[55] The Labour Party had long seemed unduly concerned with criminology rather than with crime. It placed emphasis on the social circumstances which allegedly promoted crime and which might effectively condone the actions of the criminal, rather than on the needs and rights of victims, often the least powerful and articulate members of society. The Policy Unit tried repeatedly to get Labour Party pronouncements to place more emphasis on crime and law and order issues generally, but with limited success at this period. It took the emergence of Tony Blair's leadership in 1994 to get a complete shift in attitudes—some felt to a wholly excessive degree when Jack Straw condemned street beggars whose presence offended respectable citizens and Tony Blair called, in American terms, for 'zero tolerance' towards them. Callaghan at least had an instinctive sense for what the public, including the working-class public, sought from their politicians, and how it should be expressed. He deplored a tendency in Labour ranks to discuss human and civil rights in terms of specific groups and organizations, often highly mobilized, rather than focus them in terms of the ordinary citizen, what Roosevelt called the forgotten man at the base of the economic pyramid. Callaghan wanted the forgotten man (and woman) to be restored and celebrated. Instead, to his dismay, self-interested bodies including many trade unions offered an individualistic approach that conflicted with the social cohesion and community self-discipline on which traditional British social democracy, from Keir Hardie to Jim Callaghan, fundamentally rested.

Apart from intervening at a general, philosophical, or moral level, Callaghan also intervened on a mass of individual policy themes without disturbing the general collective stance of his administration. He appreciated the space and perspective that the premiership, shorn of departmental policy responsibilities, provided. There were a variety of issues in which he took a close personal interest. One was the financing of the National Health Service. In 1977 and 1978 he intervened personally to ensure that extra expenditure was diverted to the Health Service, especially the hospital service, even at a time of public spending cuts after the IMF crisis. He compelled David Ennals, the Minister for Health and Social Security and one of the less forceful members of the Cabinet, to ensure that extra funding went to patient care rather than to the coffers of the Health Service unions.[56] The NHS, including especially the hospital service, became a priority on which he focused in 1978–9 as an election drew nearer.

Personal tax reform was another of his pet areas, drawing not only on his experience as Chancellor but on his even longer experience as a member of the Inland Revenue back in the 1930s. One remarkable aspect of prime ministerial involvement came with the question of the purchase and sale of aircraft. Callaghan became deeply implicated in this, not just as a matter of the operational policy of British Airways but as an aspect of Anglo-American relations. He immersed himself in the detail of aircraft sale and purchase in a way that astonished Bernard Donoughue and the CPRS alike. As he explained to the Commons during the Westland helicopters debate in January 1986, he was anxious that Boeing wanted 'to suck the technology out of British Aerospace and reduce its role to that of a sub-contractor'. He was also anxious about opposition in the US Congress to the use of export credits guarantees by the British government to support the sale of Rolls-Royce engines to American companies and took a robust stand in defence of British interests. He took Kenneth Berrill of the CPRS, who was chairman of the relevant interdepartmental committee, with him to Washington to discuss matters with Boeing and also with appropriate members of the US administration. The Rolls-Royce issue he took up personally with President Carter himself.[57] He also startled Norman Tebbitt, a right-wing Conservative MP who had begun life as an airline pilot, by engaging him in intimate private conversations about the details of the aerospace manufacturing industry. Tebbitt consulted his party leader about the proprieties here. Mrs Thatcher replied, 'Norman, if the prime minister wishes to speak to you, of course you must.'[58] In the event, British Aerospace, a major player in this episode, was to collaborate with the French in their airbus scheme, while Rolls-Royce co-operated with Boeing and British Airways finally chose the latter as the manufacturer of its new planes. Everybody got what they wanted. The whole affair was a remarkable case of sustained prime ministerial intervention.

In addition, Callaghan had ample scope for pressing his own policies since he was in effect in charge of foreign policy, however punctilious he was to lend moral and other support to the youthful David Owen when he succeeded Crosland at the Foreign Office in January 1977. This gave Callaghan a wide range of cards to play on many matters. They included international economic co-operation to promote recovery and liquidity, policy towards Rhodesia (where Tony Crosland tended to defer to him during his brief time as Foreign Secretary), and especially matters of defence including the future course of British nuclear policy and the prospects of a successor deterrent to replace the ageing Polaris missile system. Callaghan acted with real authority in all these areas. In addition, he undoubtedly felt that his personal links with President Ford and Dr Kissinger in the United States, until their defeat in the November 1976 presidential election, gave him extra leverage. Even more did he feel this about his strong bonds of comradeship with Chancellor Helmut Schmidt of West Germany. Like all prime ministers since 1973, he was constrained by the impact on British sovereignty of membership of the European Union. On the other hand, the fact that in 1976 the implications of membership were so uncertain and fluid perhaps gave the Prime Minister, especially as the former Foreign Secretary who had renegotiated the terms of entry, more authority in domestic politics as an interpreter of the new relationship. In the IMF crisis in November–December 1976 many Cabinet colleagues, among them Tony Benn and Edmund Dell, felt that the Prime

Minister was pursuing his own, externally directed policy by using his links with Ford and Schmidt in order to bypass the IMF to direct attention to his own favoured project of funding the sterling balances.[59] As events turned out, Callaghan's expectations were to be disappointed, even by Schmidt, and this venture into personal diplomacy was jettisoned in favour of a collective Cabinet approach. The Treasury and the Bank of England were strongly opposed. On the other hand, Callaghan's initiatives helped ensure that, with American assistance, the problem of the sterling balances was settled satisfactorily in the end.

Finally, it was in domestic economic policy that Callaghan often intervened on a personal basis. He was driven to do so after what he saw as the disastrous failures of the Heath government. From the summer of 1976, when the wages bargain with the TUC had to be renegotiated, he found himself increasingly embroiled in economic policy and often effectively in charge of it, however close his relationship with Denis Healey. His unique relationships with Len Murray of the TUC and key union leaders such as David Basnett or Tom Jackson added to his authority here. Jack Jones of the Transport Workers was more wary, but he too felt that the Prime Minister was a more sympathetic figure than his Chancellor, Denis Healey, and more committed to party unity.

At key moments, Callaghan often pursued his own course. The most remarkable instance of this, perhaps the most spectacular instance of any aspect of governmental policy between 1976 and 1979, was when he led the move away from traditional Keynesian policies and towards a modified monetarism in his speech to the Labour Party conference at Blackpool in September 1976.[60] Callaghan declared here that traditional pump-priming methods through deficit financing and public spending were no longer effective. Britain, he declared to the startled delegates, most of whom were trade unionists, could no longer spend its way out of a recession. That option no longer existed and another way must be found.

It was a bold declaration of intent to make a fresh start, and took the trade unions and the party aback. Callaghan saw it as a rejection of 'glib solutions'. Whether it was prudent or indeed wholly credible as a long-term policy is another matter. Many saw it as the Prime Minister embracing monetarism and, in effect, surrendering the ideological initiative to the Tories. It came as a surprise to Denis Healey who was not impressed by its thrust and later expressed himself pungently on the point.[61] It was largely the result of a last-minute telephone conversation between Callaghan and his economic son-in-law Peter Jay, a long-standing critic in the press of orthodox Keynesianism and an apostle of monetary discipline and cash limits.[62] How rigorous a break with traditional Keynesian ideas Callaghan meant this speech to be is open to debate. He himself was to reject some of the more apocalyptic interpretations of it later on, such as that it was an anticipation of the views of Milton Friedman and the Chicago monetarist school. He regarded himself as still a Keynesian but one who recognized the limits of the ideas of the master,[63] who after all had worked out his theories no less than forty years earlier. His speech was intended to focus on the particular problem confronting discussions with the IMF rather than suggest a general recasting of British economic management. It brought enthusiastic praise from one right-wing Labour economist, Lord Vaizey, who praised his 'GREAT speech at Blackpool'.[64] But the view of this recently ennobled peer, a beneficiary of Harold Wilson's final honours list, was a minority one at the time.

But the speech also caused political and industrial difficulties for him. The discussions with the unions on wage norms were made the more difficult, quite apart from the virtual ungovernability of some of the major unions such as NUPE. Prime ministerial appeals for wage restraint were met with bitter complaints by workers in the Health Service or local government who felt that they had borne the brunt of severe retrenchment in public expenditure from 1976. Callaghan's conference speech then suggested, perhaps, the dangers as well as the potentialities of prime ministerial policy initiatives. On balance, though, Callaghan seized his opportunities for individual action shrewdly, at least down to September 1978, and in a way that strengthened both his administration and his personal authority. In the 'winter of discontent', by contrast, a series of errors led both into an irreversible phase of decline.

In his views of the system of governance more generally, Callaghan reflected current orthodoxy and was relatively conservative. There was no need to change matters fundamentally since he had all the levers of power at his disposal and his authority was effectively untrammelled. That did not mean that he could not be innovative. The most notable instance of this was to be the 'seminar' on economic policy spearheaded by Harold Lever in 1977–8. Chaired by the Prime Minister, it included the Chancellor of the Exchequer, the Foreign Secretary, the Governor and Deputy Governor of the Bank of England, Bernard Donoughue, Sir John Hunt, Kenneth Berrill, Kenneth Stowe, and a few others, and took a broad overview of fiscal and monetary policy, especially in relation to that of other countries. Callaghan felt the Treasury was constrained by seeing matters in terms of day-to-day management. The seminar met on 5 July 1977 to discuss the reserves and interest rates; on 20 October 1977 to look at inflows of foreign currency which were endangering the Chancellor's M3 monetary targets; on 6 March 1978 to consider the 'dollar initiative' (Harold Lever wanted the dollar to be a new reserve currency); and on 7 November 1978 to examine monetary policy including a new target range for M3, the broad money supply.[65] It may be taken as an important additional forum for considering modifications of Keynesian policies. In a Fabian inquiry in 1980 Gavyn Davies was to criticize it sharply for bypassing the Cabinet and making collective responsibility 'a sham'. But this is surely an error. The seminar was merely that—a forum for discussion of long-term issues in an informal way, not an instrument for any kind of decision-making. It could well be argued that it brought ministers in to debate matters that would otherwise be discussed in secrecy with the Governor and officials of the Bank of England. They could not be discussed in full Cabinet—for one thing, it was believed that some ministers might immediately leak them to MPs or journalists. The seminar was just simply an occasional medium for stimulating discussion—Callaghan notes in his memoirs that fourteen meetings only were held in 1977–8, and his notes confirm the point—rather than any attempt to bypass the formal machinery for the conduct of economic and fiscal policy. It also enabled the Prime Minister to receive information and advice from key figures like Gordon Richardson and Kit McMahon, the Governor and Deputy Governor of the Bank of England, at first hand rather than have it mediated through the Treasury whose secretive approach the Prime Minister knew and resented.[66]

Otherwise, Callaghan, like Clement Attlee before him, did not leave a legacy of constitutional innovation. Harold Wilson did attempt reforms of the civil service and the House of Lords but they yielded little; the first national referendum conducted in 1975 was his one remarkably successful novelty. (On balance Labour's most adventurous prime minister in this regard may be considered to be Ramsay MacDonald, even if some of his innovations were forced on him by financial catastrophe in 1931.) Callaghan felt that the civil service worked well and efficiently and was a model for other nations. There was no need to tamper with it. The 'elephantine' Civil Service Department (to use Bernard Donoughue's term)[67] was left alone and it was to be Mrs Thatcher who abolished it in 1981. The other reforms proposed by the Fulton Committee in the 1960s were left dormant. A major criticism offered by Labour of the civil service machine was that it was ideologically biased in favour of continuity and that Labour's own advisers were left on the outside. However, with McNally and his Political Office and Donoughue and the Policy Unit, Callaghan felt that he had ample sources of appropriate party advice, while others could be brought in by ministers as Roy Hattersley had enlisted the aid of David Hill.

On balance, Callaghan took a stern and purist view as all prime ministers, other than Lloyd George and perhaps Churchill, had done before him, that political advisers and career civil servants should be kept in separate compartments. He strongly disapproved of the later policy of Mrs Thatcher which appeared to blur the line and to suck diplomats like Sir Anthony Parsons and Sir Crispin Tickell or civil service advisers such as Charles Powell into her personal political machine. Like all his Labour predecessors and most of his Cabinet colleagues (Tony Benn, the apostle of open government, being a conspicuous and vocal exception) Callaghan felt that the civil service should be left alone. It should stay unpoliticized, confidential, and non-partisan. As a senior figure in 1996 he was to speak out robustly in support of his former private secretary at the Treasury, Lord Bancroft, in condemning the 'letting out' of civil service posts on an agency basis. On other areas, he was equally cautious. The reform of local government had been undertaken by the Heath government in 1972–3 and Callaghan, while he disapproved of some aspects of it, saw no reason to tamper with so recent a structure. On Scottish and Welsh devolution, he felt that changes in this direction were a necessary evil, to placate the Scottish Nationalists and Plaid Cymru members in the House on whose support he partly depended, rather than something constitutionally desirable. He ploughed the sands of Celtic devolution in the later 1970s without enthusiasm or great commitment.

The House of Lords he also left on one side, mindful, as he told Douglas Houghton, of how he had burnt his fingers on the issue when Wilson proposed to reform its composition in 1968.[68] The fact that it often intervened inconveniently for his minority government, for instance rejecting government schemes for further nationalization or planning agreements, did not cause him undue pain. In the 1979 election manifesto he made sure that proposals by Eric Heffer for abolishing the upper house or, alternatively, making it an elective body, with the hereditary peers abolished, were cut out. Of the upper house in general he had a low opinion. He quoted Macmillan with approval as someone who had refused a peerage (of course, Macmillan later changed his mind and became Lord Stockton) and cited the former Conservative premier as someone who spoke with contempt of appearing in a minor provincial music hall after 'treading the boards at Drury Lane'. He told Cledwyn Hughes in February 1978 that he would not take a peerage after he retired. He would prefer to commute from his farm to take seminars in Sussex University and thus have the company of intelligent young people 'and not the old fogies who frequented the Lords'.[69] When he did in fact become a peer years later in 1987 it was simply to remain to some degree active in front-line politics. He had no particular admiration for the upper house even if no wish either to reform or modernize it. Again it was not until the mid-1990s that Labour was to make constitutional change a policy priority. Tony Blair was now personally committed to reforming the House of Lords, along with Scottish and Welsh devolution (on a PR basis) and a bill of rights. But over the years, compared with the handling of the Lords by the Liberals Asquith and Lloyd George, or even the Conservative Harold Macmillan, Labour governments have been restrained as constitutional innovators.

In one important area, Callaghan was highly traditionalist. He fully conformed to the pattern of the monarch's having generally better relations with Labour prime ministers than with Conservative ones. With Edward Heath, the relations of Queen Elizabeth were 'correct but cool'.[70] In terms of laying on compliments with a trowel for his sovereign (or, indeed, any woman) Heath fell a long way short of Disraeli. The Queen did not warm to Heath's somewhat glacial personality and disapproved of his coolness towards the Commonwealth as opposed to his obsessive enthusiasm for Europe. With Mrs Thatcher later on, the relationship, according to most accounts, was relatively frosty, with the Commonwealth again an area of indirect conflict, including the issue of sanctions on South Africa. The British right wing did not enjoy their Queen sharing a Christmas Day broadcast with Mrs Indira Gandhi.[71] By contrast, the Queen got on well with Harold Wilson whom she found human and amusing, in a gossipy way; the *New Statesman* once described him as 'the working man's Melbourne'. Callaghan also had an excellent relationship with the Queen whom he not only respected as monarch but greatly liked as a person. They got on well enough for the Prime Minister to compliment his sovereign on occasion for her dress sense. On Commonwealth and other matters, they were clearly of one mind. He derived personal pleasure from leading the national celebrations of the monarch's silver jubilee in 1977. This led to a lengthy discussion in the Cabinet about an appropriate form of present to the Queen. Shirley Williams proposed a saddle, Tony Benn a vase carved in coal by a Polish miner, and Lord Elwyn-Jones a Welsh clock. In the end, the Prime Minister authorized Audrey to buy a silver coffee-pot. The weekly royal audiences were genial and relaxed, with conversation ranging easily over a variety of topics, political and personal. The Queen was quick to offer her moral support on difficult occasions such as in the renewal of talks with Ian Smith to try to find a settlement in Rhodesia. By contrast, the Duke of Edinburgh, despite the shared naval background which Callaghan respected, had come to be regarded as a somewhat loose cannon, sometimes tactless and maladroit in giving his (usually reactionary) opinions on public issues.[72]

One of the areas to which Callaghan devoted some attention was in trying to find a meaningful role for the Prince of Wales. Indeed, as a Cardiff MP, Callaghan had already had a good deal of contact with Prince Charles on various Welsh public occasions; the Prince, for instance, became in 1977 chancellor of the University of Wales from which the Prime Minister had the previous year received an honorary degree and whose gatherings he often attended. They were to be thrown together much more in the future when Callaghan became president of the University College of Swansea (renamed in 1994 the University of Wales, Swansea). During his premiership, Callaghan devoted some effort to trying to find Charles 'a proper job', as the phrase went, and tried to instruct him in the processes of government. The Prince attended NEDO, toured 10 Downing Street, and on one occasion attended a meeting of the Cabinet. Callaghan also tried to interest the Prince in the activities of the private office, notably in the preparations for prime minister's question time. Mrs Thatcher was startled, and perhaps angered, when he turned up for this gladiatorial event in the House with relatively little warning. The relationship of the premier to the young Prince was avuncular and usually amiable. But it was also 'widely believed', as the royal biographer, Jonathan Dimbleby, correctly writes, that Callaghan was disappointed by the relative lack of interest the Prince took in political affairs, as compared to his various private enthusiasms for classical architecture, holistic religions, correct English, and organic farming. One important civil service aide, otherwise discreet, sharply criticized the Prince in private as 'an arrogant young man' in offering a disdainful lack of response to Callaghan's efforts to give him a meaningful training in public affairs. Apparently Prince Charles cited the view of Lord Home that his public duties as Prince of Wales were quite taxing enough without his having to involve himself in time-consuming administrative work. Possible membership of the Commonwealth Development Corporation met with the same negative and complacent attitude.

When the marriage of the Prince and Princess Diana came to an effective end in the mid-1990s, Callaghan was foremost amongst those asking for an early divorce so that the private breakdown of a marriage did not lead to a public debate on the future of the monarchy.[73] He did not want a historic institution put in jeopardy by the wayward behaviour of the heir to the throne and his glamorous but capricious wife. As Prime Minister, he set his face against attempts to weaken the authority or prestige of the Crown. Pressure from some in the Labour Party, notably Tony Benn, for the Civil List to be cut down if not abolished, and the Queen to lose her immunity to taxation on her vast income, was stoutly resisted, as it had been by Wilson before him. Like all Labour leaders since the time of Keir Hardie (who had famously derided the birth of the future Edward VIII at the time of a Welsh mining disaster),[74] Jim Callaghan was no constitutional radical and no republican.

The other aspects of the prime ministerial role, apart from his leadership of the Cabinet and the governmental machine, lay in his activities as party leader and as communicator and image-maker with the general public. With the party, as will be seen, Callaghan had constant difficulty. As Prime Minister he was uniquely preoccupied in devising ways of keeping the parliamentary party, the National Executive, the Cabinet, Transport House, and the unions in some kind of harmony, or, in the cliché of the time, singing from the same hymn sheet. In handling the PLP, for all the revolts that occurred on a variety of issues, he was remarkably effective. As he always had done, he spent much time in the Commons tearoom, hobnobbing with Labour backbenchers, soliciting their views, and taking a keen and genuine interest in their personal circumstances and problems. He spent more time with Welsh members than he had tended to do in the past: with Welshmen like Ted Rowlands, Brynmor Jones, Alan Williams, and Donald Coleman occupying key middle-ranking posts in the administration, there was talk of a Welsh 'Taffia' emerging as under Lloyd George. Unlike many prime ministers, he regularly lunched in the Commons dining-room, choosing his dining companions at random amongst Labour backbenchers. They mostly felt that they knew him and many had affectionate tales to tell afterwards.

The National Executive was far less amenable. Even for one of his prestige and dominance, especially since his links with the unions after his election as party treasurer in 1967, he had endless trouble as the NEC marched resolutely and almost unthinkingly to the left. Tom McNally's account of meetings with the NEC/TUC Liaison Committee, and of sessions of the National Executive from his first meeting with Geoff Bish and David Lea, of Transport House and the TUC respectively, from 11 May 1976 onwards, were a saga of the party's representatives failing to recognize the economic difficulties confronting the nation, ignoring the pressure of inflation, and pushing on with ever more costly social and economic projects. Callaghan had to rebut some of the immediate proposals, such as a 'generous' child benefit scheme to be introduced early in 1977. He minuted

McNally, 'Can you find some "costless" social projects? e.g. What about B.D.'s paper on selling council houses?' McNally replied that almost all the proposals would mean public expenditure, other than 'in the industrial democracy and machinery of government field'.[75] The Chancellor was quick to observe that a combination of labour subsidies and training programmes, the planning agreements with 100 leading companies, funding for the National Enterprise Board, a ceiling for the penetration of imports, a commitment to 150m. tons of coal output by the mid-1980s, a wealth tax, a proposal for half of average earnings for retirement pensions for married couples, higher child allowances, and community ownership of rented property would all cost much money at a time of severe economic difficulties. There was also a failure to acknowledge that these would mean swingeing tax increases at a time when working people had suffered cuts in their living standards for two to three years. Higher public expenditure in any case would compete with the vital demands of exports and industrial investment.[76] On a later occasion, Gavyn Davies pointed out the dangers of Labour's increases in public spending. Whereas the Tories planned a decrease of 2.7 per cent, Labour had increased it by 8.6 per cent, and indeed three times faster than gross national product.[77]

Callaghan fully endorsed all these criticisms, and various arguments with the NEC resulted. The belief of members of the National Executive that the government was deliberately marginalizing them raised the temperature still further. Barbara Castle was often an embittered critic in these meetings. Her proposal on 24 September to condemn the government for its spending cuts was tied 14 : 14, with Michael Foot and (under orders) Tony Benn supporting the government's view. Only the casting vote of the chairman of the NEC, Tom Bradley, prevented a conflict between party and government. McNally reported that the bitterness of Barbara Castle's 'attempt to make personal political capital' had alienated even some on the left but this kind of tension continued for the rest of Callaghan's premiership.[78] Her dogmatic, self-absorbed style annoyed some of her former admirers. On the other hand, she could very reasonably respond that she was speaking out in defence of the policies in Labour's 1974 election manifestos, whereas Callaghan and his aides were casting them aside.

As the swing to the left in the constituency parties and many of the unions went on, Callaghan's difficulties in keeping a hold over his party were compounded. This was sharply reflected in his problem in controlling the parliamentary party during the IMF talks in December 1976. The greatest machine operator of his time, he found that a newly radicalized, if diminished, party rejected the government's calls for moderation and consensus. The IMF crisis did not end the arguments since a feeling that at least Callaghan had averted a crisis of 1931 proportions was balanced by anger at the spending cuts and growing unemployment that followed. Demands for a siege economy continued unabated. On one issue after another, proposals by the Prime Minister, the Chancellor, and the great majority of the Cabinet for wage restraint, economic caution, and an end to proposals that, as Harold Lever put it, 'merely alarm business opinion at home and abroad' were rebuffed.[79] A typical episode was the presentation of a Liaison Committee document on July 1977. McNally reported the Policy Unit's view that it contained 'no serious discussion of inflation'.[80] On the other side, left-wing figures on the NEC such as Mikardo, Frank Allaun, and Joan Maynard, abetted by younger figures such as Neil Kinnock and Denis Skinner, and by union leaders such as Clive Jenkins of ASTMS and Alan Fisher of NUPE, pressed on with their own agenda— more socialism, a planned if not a siege economy, the nationalization of banks and insurance companies, the conscription of private funds and a wealth tax, minimal ties with Europe, and an end to the British nuclear deterrent. Tom McNally was to describe the Executive as dominated by ideologues. In Transport House, the national agent, Reg Underhill, was tired and dispirited. The general secretary, Ron Hayward, a leftish figure, was 'obsessed with pelf and peace', while key organizers like Geoff Bish and Jenny Little were mainly anxious to work with the left.[81]

It was clear, long before Callaghan fell from office in May 1979, that a sea change was occurring in the labour movement. The consensual ethos for which Callaghan had always stood—the famous 'broad church' view of the Labour Party—was, for the moment at least, in total abeyance. Callaghan had two choices. One was to engage in an all-out confrontation with the party left, in effect fight in a civil war more brutal even than that between Gaitskellites and Bevanites in the early 1950s, to purge the left of its influence. One signal of this would have been to act on the Underhill report on 'entryism' in the constituency parties by Trotskyist elements, Militant Tendency, and others on the furthest left fringe. Even had Callaghan been younger than his mid-sixties, it is unlikely that he would have been able to deflect himself from his wider role as Prime Minister. Nor did Healey, Crosland, Foot, or other key ministers show any sign of wanting him to do so. In any case, in the current mood of the party, any such attempt would certainly have failed. The other course was to soldier on, appealing to the mass public and the community at large over the heads of unrepresentative and doctrinaire constituency activists as a national leader, symbolizing the unity of the nation as a whole, and this is what Callaghan by instinct and by ideology attempted to do.

Here he was on much stronger ground. One opinion poll after another throughout the period 1976–9 showed that his reputation was high and often rising with the general public. His standing as Prime Minister went up as that of Labour as the party preference of the voters steadily went down. Down to May 1979, his standing with the voters was far higher than that of Margaret Thatcher, the Opposition leader, though gender prejudice may have contributed to the poor ratings that she achieved prior to entering No. 10. Some of his advisers in the 1979 election campaign pressed hard for a televised presidential-style debate with her, convinced that this would result in an overwhelming triumph for their man which would snatch an improbable last-minute Labour victory. He dominated her with some ease at prime minister's question time, aided by more than a trace of patronizing contempt shown by male backbenchers for a 'handbag swinging' (or even menopausal) female opponent. Hugo Young has criticized Callaghan's approach to Margaret Thatcher as offensive and 'extraordinarily condescending'.[82] But the premier was equally effective in handling male critics. Nigel Lawson had been an effective and sometimes damaging interrogator of Harold Wilson during prime minister's question time. Callaghan proved 'very much harder to deal with' and Lawson then gave up.[83] On television and in public appearances, Callaghan appeared as a genial and relaxed figure, avuncular, reassuring, embodying the old values of neighbourhood, family, and an orderly and law-abiding society. He became skilled in combating the probing of television interviewers, even those as robust as Robin Day, with whom he had some passages of arms. Usually his appearances on *Panorama*, *The World at Ten*, and similar programmes went well and strengthened his appeal with the electors. One or two Cabinet colleagues, however, felt that in television interviews he would appear too 'grumpy'.[84] Off camera, he could be sharper still. Overall, however, his public image was a strong one. Willie Whitelaw and other Tory leaders feared that a Labour victory in the next general election might see Callaghan build up a personal hegemony of a formidable and perhaps unbeatable kind.

More generally, he was a patriot of an old-fashioned type, whether in his attitude to British institutions or to British possessions such as Gibraltar or the Falklands. His naval background undoubtedly played a part in this, too. He felt thoroughly at home during the royal jubilee in 1977. Invariably, he offered an imperturbable image of British sang-froid and common sense. But this was not always in conformity with reality. Journalists and associates could find him in private to be alarmingly bad-tempered, when the public image of 'Sunny Jim' gave way to thunderous outbursts. One leading television journalist, trying to arrange an interview, even alleged that he had his professional future threatened as a result. One journalist on a quality Sunday newspaper was deeply hostile, using terms like 'thug', and 'bully' and speculating that Callaghan would have been at home in Nazi Germany.[85] But these cases were not typical and most members of the press usually found him amiable and considerate.

Some of these temperamental vagaries, anyhow, must have been the result of the extreme pressures to which any prime minister was subjected. Many others found the Prime Minister reassuring in his approachability and humanity. This was particularly the viewpoint of his constituents and party associates in Cardiff and in Wales in general, which he came to embrace as never before. In the past, he had tended to be seen in Wales as essentially an English spokesman for the Anglicized south-east. This, however, may have reflected the historic social and political divide between Welsh and Anglicized Wales: somewhat similar charges were later made against Neil Kinnock, undoubtedly a proud Welshman with a Welsh-speaking wife, but a man from the Gwent border country never-theless. Callaghan sometimes attended the national eisteddfod and, as a working farmer, hugely enjoyed the Royal Welsh Show each July. As an old player himself, he made good use of the great success of the Welsh rugby team during his years as premier. The 'triple crown' team of 1978 was invited to 10 Downing Street for a reception, which was a highly popular move.[86] On balance, Callaghan offered a good public front for the British people. He was an excellent communicator in parliament and on the plat-form, and offered a solid, honest façade after the tensions of the Wilson era. As noted, he won widespread respect from overseas associates as well, in the United States and the Commonwealth, but also increasingly in Europe. Callaghan as Prime Minister was a highly effective image-maker, but he was the more successful because the image seemed to conform to the reality. He was amongst the most credible of populists.

James Callaghan's premiership offered a supreme challenge. It was one that he took up with aplomb and general success. He enjoyed a credibility and standing throughout his time as premier, even during the last difficult phase of the 'winter of discontent', which he had never enjoyed in public office before. He appeared to have made the transition successfully from party politician and machine operator to national and international states-man, and the reputation stuck thereafter. In many ways, perhaps, the pre-miership was the most appropriate position for his particular combination of talents. His main skills had always lain in strategic or global decision-making rather than the technical details of departmental policy. He had not, in that sense, ever been a willing technocrat, nor had he led Labour initiatives in individual areas of policy. As Prime Minister, he could stand back and reflect, and weigh up the options in a mood of some serenity and confidence. He felt himself to be, as Attlee had not, significantly more than *primus inter pares* in the administration. He noted how he appeared to have more time on his hands in No. 10, to stand back, to think, and to lead. The Cabinet Secretary admired his capacity to concentrate on a few salient issues such as pay policy or SALT II. He could leave the practicalities of implementing government policy to others, and remain himself detached and above the mêlée. He was a slow, deliberate reader of Cabinet papers. Bernard Donoughue noted how his style was to pace himself, to take his time and assess a problem in all its aspects, rather than hurl himself into the minutiae of individual areas as Harold Wilson, an intellectually more agile premier, tended to do.[87]

It was a sober, measured style, but one that brought some reassurance to a party and nation sorely tried by the disturbing pressures of the 1970s, the financial crisis brought about by the fourfold rise in the price of oil, the rising unemployment and spiralling inflation, the tension in labour relations, and the growing signs of violence in social, neighbourhood, and family life. The 1970s were a troubled, anguished time for the British people. It is not surprising that this decade has received the somewhat dubious accolade of being 'the golden age of criminology'.[88] It threw up class, ethnic, generational, and eventually gender tensions on a scale hitherto unparalleled in British history. From mass picketing to football hooligans to battered wives cowering in women's refuges, there were mounting signs of a far more violent society than in the immediate post-war years. In the Thatcher period, the indices for crime were to become far worse. It was perhaps as well in all this turmoil that Britain produced a prime minister as measured and urbane in style as James Callaghan. Two decades on, Blairite image-makers like Peter Mandelson would regard him as a dated figure, the epitome of 'Old Labour' rooted in the working class and the links with the unions.[89] For many contemporaries in the late 1970s, that was just what a troubled nation required. One Labour veteran, at least, was well pleased, and his view perhaps was not unrepresentative. Lord Noel-Baker told him in October 1977 that 'Lots of people, Liberals, Conservatives, journalists, say to me that you have become a great prime minister. So you have. Carry on!'[90]

1. L. J. Callaghan, *The Political Leader*, with a foreword by Senator Walter Mondale (Minneapolis, 1982), 21. Other observations of his on these themes appear in 'James Callaghan: The Stateman as CEO', an interview by Alan M. Webber, *Harvard Business Review* (Nov.–Dec. 1986), 106–12.

2. Information from Sir Reginald Hibbert; Norman Tebbitt, *Upwardly Mobile* (London, 1989), 196—'given time and excuse he would always prevaricate'; interview with Tony Blair, *New Statesman*, 5 July 1996.

3. Wilson to Callaghan, 27 Apr. 1976 (Callaghan Papers, uncatalogued).

4. Bernard Donoughue, *Prime Minister* (London, 1988), 30.

5. Hunt to Callaghan, 15 July 1976 (Callaghan Papers, box 22).

6. Hunt memo, 2 July 1976 (ibid. box 19).

7. Hunt memos, 16 Dec. 1976, 6 Jan. 1977 (ibid., box 19). At a later discussion between Callaghan and Lord Armstrong, 26 Oct. 1977 (ibid., box 19), it was agreed that the idea was impractical.

8. Memo, ? 1977 (Callaghan Papers, box 19); Tony Benn, *Conflicts of Interest: Diaries, 1977–80* (London, 1990), 172 (21 June 1977); Donoughue, *Prime Minister*, 146.

9. Lord Hunt, 'Cabinet Government in the Mid to Late 1970s', *Contemporary Record*, 8/3 (winter 1994), 467 ff.

10. On this, see John Turner, *Lloyd George's Secretariat* (Cambridge, 1980).

11. Stowe memo, 'Initiatives', 28 Apr. 1976 (Callaghan Papers, box 19).

12. Interview with Sir Kenneth Stowe; Prime Minister's diary (ibid., box 35).

13. Interview with Lord Callaghan; memo by Nigel Wicks (ibid.).

14. Interview with Sir Bryan Cartledge.

15. See Tessa Blackstone and William Plowden, *Inside the Think Tank: Advising the Cabinet, 1971–1983* (London, 1988).

16. Ibid. 56–7.

17. Tessa Blackstone, 'Education for 16- to 19-Year-Olds: Some Proposals for Change', in M. Williams, R. Daugherty, and F. Banks (eds.), *Continuing the Education Debate* (London, 1992), 86.

18. Donoughue minute on 'The Family', 9 June 1978 (private papers); *Sunday Times*, 28 May 1978, supplement on 'The Family'.

19. Material in Callaghan Papers.

20. Interview with Lord Donoughue.

21. Cledwyn Hughes diary, 23 July 1976.

22. Donoughue paper, 'Themes and Initiatives' (PU 175), 16 Apr. 1976 (Callaghan Papers, box 19).

23. Material ibid.; Donoughue, *Prime Minister*, 21.

24. Berrill to Donoughue, 15 Dec. 1976; Donoughue to Berrill, 17 Dec. 1976; Berrill to Donoughue, 24 Dec. 1976; Gavyn Davies note to the Prime Minister, 11 Jan. 1977 (Callaghan Papers, box 9).

25. e.g. 'Mr. Benn's Paper on Import Controls' (PU 236), 26 Nov. 1976 (ibid., box 13). Donoughue comments that Benn 'offers a bogus choice between a caricature of the IMF route and an unrealistically rosy alternative strategy'. He went on that 'Benn seems to think that the EEC would be willing to allow us to impose controls and then lend us money. This is most unlikely.'

26. Gavyn Davies, 'The Medium Term Asessment', 17 June 1977 (PU 284) (Callaghan

Papers, box 9). This paper concluded that the government should bring forward reflation as soon as possible and delay the election for as long as possible.

27. Donoughue memo, 'Thoughts on the Government's Future Strategy' (PU 281), 2 June 1977 (private papers).

28. Donoughue memo, 6 July 1977 (PU 289) (ibid.). This was in part an argument for the early implementation of child benefit paid direct to mothers.

29. Donoughue memo, 9 and 26 Sept. 1977 (PU 303, 306) (ibid.).

30. Donoughue memo, 'Themes and Initiatives' (PU 390), 14 Sept. 1978; Donoughue to Callaghan, 19 Sept. 1978 (private papers).

31. Donoughue memo, 'Last Three Days'. ? May 1979 (ibid., box 23).

32. Interview with Tom McNally.

33. Minute from McNally, 26 Apr. 1976 (Callaghan Papers, box 22).

34. McNally to Stowe, 21 Sept. 1976 (ibid.).

35. Interview with Sir Tom McCaffrey; Donoughue, *Prime Minister*, 25.

36. Interviews with Tom McNally and Sir Tom McCaffrey.

37. Robert Harris, *Good and Faithful Servant* (London, 1990), 67.

38. Owen, *Time to Declare*, 323.

39. Benn, *Office without Power*, 557 (12 Apr. 1976).

40. Private information.

41. Cledwyn Hughes diary, 31 March 1977.

42. Interview with Michael Callaghan.

43. Callaghan memo to ministers (Callaghan Papers, box 19).

44. Interview with Lord Rodgers.

45. Interview with Michael Foot.

46. Material in Callaghan Papers, box 19; interview with Roy Hattersley.

47. See memos on this by the Policy Unit, Callaghan Papers, box 13.

48. Cledwyn Hughes diary, 23 Feb. 1978.

49. Interview with Lord Healey.

50. Healey, *The Time of my Life*, 447 ff.

51. See n. 22 above; McNally memo, 30 Apr. 1976 (Callaghan Papers, box 22).

52. Callaghan, *Time and Chance*, 409.

53. Various drafts in the Callaghan Papers. It was printed in *Education*, 22 Oct. 1976, in full. Blackstone, 'Education for 16- to 19-Year-Olds', says that civil servants, HM inspectors, and others were 'not too happy with Jim's splendid initiative'.

54. This theme appeared in Callaghan's first television broadcast as Prime Minister. The Policy Unit was anxious to distinguish between this approach and 'Thatcherism' and advocated a policy of 'tough honesty' which combined an emphasis on responsibility with a philosophy of reform and compassion for the disadvantaged (Donoughue memo, PU 175, Callaghan Papers, box 19).

55. *Castle Diaries, 1974–76*, 182 (16 Sept. 1974); Callaghan speech to WRVS, 25 Apr. 1978; Callaghan note on Home Policy Committee Papers, 2 Nov. 1977 (Callaghan Papers, box 23).

56. Donoughue, *Prime Minister*, 114.

57. Blackstone and Plowden, *Inside the Think Tank*, 141; interview with Lord Donoughue; see Callaghan's speech in Westland debate, *Parl. Deb.*, 6th ser., vol. 89, 1110–11 (15 Jan. 1986).

58. Tebbitt, *Upwardly Mobile*, 196.

59. Cf. Kathy Burk and Alec Cairncross, 'Goodbye Great Britain' (London, 1992), 91–4.

60. *Financial Times*, 29 Sept. 1976.

61. Interview with Lord Healey. The word 'crap' was used.

62. 'Message for Philip Wood from Mrs Jay', 25 Sept. 1976 (private papers).

63. Interviews with Lord Callaghan and Peter Jay.

64. Lord Vaizey to Callaghan, 1 Oct. 1976 (Callaghan Papers, box 9).

65. Donoughue memo (PU 287), 4 July 1977; Donoughue memo, 'The Economic Seminar' (PU 309), 14 Oct. 1977; Donoughue memo, 'The Dollar Initiative' (PU 364), 3 Mar. 1978 and Gavyn Davies's paper on 'The Dollar Seminar', ? 1978; and Donoughue memo (PU 397), 7 Nov. 1978 (private papers).

66. *Time and Chance*, 476; for Gavyn Davies's criticisms, see Peter Hennessy, *Cabinet* (Oxford, 1986), 92.

67. Donoughue, *Prime Minister*, 27.

68. Callaghan to Houghton, 20 May 1977 (Callaghan Papers, box 9).

69. Cledwyn Hughes diary, 9 Feb. 1978.

70. Campbell, *Edward Hearth*, 493–4.

71. Hugo Young, *One of Us* (London, 1989), 498 ff.

72. Note of a conversation with Michael Adeane, 27 May 1969 (Callaghan Papers, uncatalogued). For an interesting discussion of Callaghan's relations with the Queen, see Ben Pimlott, *The Queen* (London, 1996), 433–5.

73. Jonathan Dimbleby, *The Prince of Wales* (London, 1994), 229; Lord Callaghan, article in *Evening Standard*, Nov. 1995.

74. Kenneth O. Morgan, *Keir Hardie, Radical and Socialist* (London, 1974), 71.

75. McNally to Callaghan and Callaghan note, 11 May 1976 (Callaghan Papers, box 9).

76. K. Couzens (private secretary to the Chancellor) to Callaghan, 21 May 1976 (ibid.).

77. Gavyn Davies, 'Public Expenditure: Conservative and Labour Plans', 22 Nov. 1976 (Callaghan Papers, box 13).

78. *Financial Times*, 25 Sept. 1976; McNally to Callaghan, 15 Sept. 1976 (Callaghan Papers, box 17).

79. Memo from Harold Lever, 9 June 1976 (Callaghan Papers, box 9).

80. McNally to Callaghan, 22 July 1977 (ibid.).

81. McCaffrey memo, 24 June 1977 (Callaghan Papers, box 19).

82. *The Scotsman* survey, just before polling day in May 1979, showed Callaghan with a rating of 46% and Mrs Thatcher with one of 33%. However, Mrs Thatcher led amongst women voters. Also see Young, *One of Us*, 123. Cf. Margaret Thatcher, *The Path to Power* (London, 1995), 313, that Callaghan's manner towards her was 'patronizing and made it hard for me to advance serious criticism of Government policy without appearing to nag'. She had her revenge by never inviting him back to Chequers, whereas John Major invited him early on to an informal buffet lunch when he was shown his window in the Long Gallery. Callaghan commented, 'I had never seen it because Mrs Thatcher never asked me back here' (*The Times*, 18 Mar. 1991).

83. Lawson, *The View from No.11*, 12.

84. Private information.

85. Private information.

86. Prime Minister's diary, 1978 (Callaghan Papers, box 35); information from Mr Ray Gravell, former centre three-quarter in the Welsh team.

87. Interview with Lord Hunt of Tanworth; Donoughue, *Prime Minister*, 12.

88. Paul Rock (ed.), *A History of British Criminology* (Oxford, 1988), 61–2.

89. Peter Mandelson and Roger Liddle, *The Blair Revolution* (London, 1996).

90. Lord Noel-Baker to Callaghan, 7 Oct. 1977 (Callaghan Papers, box 9).

24

A SUCCESSFUL GOVERNMENT

THE Callaghan government has been a victim of disinformation. It has not exactly been written out of history as the Heath administration commonly was by supporters of Mrs Thatcher and hammers of the 'one-nation' 'wets' in the 1980s. It has rather been misrepresented by being recalled solely in terms of the initial crisis of the IMF negotiations and the culminating *Götterdämmerung* of the winter of discontent. This is less than half the story. Most of it has still to be written.

Historians should, of course, give due attention to the Cabinet's divisions in the autumn of 1976. They should emphasize also the industrial and political collapse that saw the Callaghan government almost humiliatingly thrust from power. But stories have a middle as well as a beginning and an end. The administration was to last in all three years and one month. For twenty of those thirty-seven months, more than half its length, from January 1977 to September 1978 the government showed many signs of being politically and economically successful. It was far from being simply an interlude. This appeared to be the most thriving period that Britain had known since the heyday of Harold Macmillan in the later 1950s. The Opposition under Mrs Thatcher seemed relatively ineffective. The year 1977 in particular was an *annus mirabilis*, with Callaghan's presidency of the European Community and successful chairing of the Commonwealth prime ministers' and NATO meetings, and the economic summit in London, along with ample photo-opportunities during the royal jubilee. James Callaghan achieved an authority as Prime Minister that astonished many close observers of his long career. Labour showed real signs of being not just in office but in power.

It is important, therefore, to avoid the kind of reductionism of some later accounts and to give proper weight to the effective record of the Callaghan government for most of its time in office. Historians of the Social Democrats after 1981 have, perhaps understandably, been remiss in not giving a properly balanced account of the Callaghan years,[1] as they appeared to contemporaries at the time and as they relate to the broader history of *fin de siècle* Britain. They were only in part a time of crisis and decline. They were also, to borrow from early American history, an 'era of good feelings' and a credible advertisement for Labour as a party of government. Some evangelists for New Labour in the 1990s, who wrote off the late 1970s as the death-pangs of an old corporatist order, failed to acknowledge that it was then that many of their party's social and economic policies were modernized and redefined.

The basis of the recovery in the government's fortunes lay in the great improvement in the economy once the IMF crisis was safely negotiated. The new year opened with news on 1 January that the pound was enjoying better health. It had risen to $1.70, thirteen points above its lowest point in relation to a basket of other currencies in late October. Tony Benn, as Minister for Energy, brought the glad tidings that the flow of oil from the North Sea was going on apace, with exports of top-quality crude increasing rapidly and huge potential savings on the balance of payments (£2,000m. was the figure commonly quoted).[2] By 1980 Britain, uniquely among all the western powers, would be self-sufficient in oil. The announcement by Denis Healey on 11 January of the agreement with the IMF and central banks to 'achieve an orderly reduction in the role of sterling as a reserve currency' was enthusiastically received in international money markets, as was a $1.5 bn. loan with European banks negotiated by the Bank of England to achieve this rundown. As Callaghan had prophesied, removing this crucial aspect of the vulnerability of sterling and ending the exposed position of the sterling balances had a strong impact on the national finances. There were massive inflows of foreign capital, both into sterling and into gilt-edged securities, amounting to $2 bn. for the month of January. On 28 January, minimum lending rate was cut by 1 per cent to 12.25 per cent, the biggest cut since the old bank rate was changed in 1972. This was only the start; twelve months later it was to stand at 8.5 per cent.[3] Small businesses and mortgaged home owners, the vulnerable vanguard of the beleaguered suburban middle class, rejoiced. At last Britain was hearing some good economic news with every expectation that it would last.

As the economy improved, so did the standing of the Prime Minister, even if his party continued to show up badly in the opinion polls. Journalists had been generally negative towards his performance until the completion of the talks with the IMF in early December. They were wont to compare his apparently brief administration with those of Douglas-

Home in 1963–4, or even of the lachrymose and hapless Lord Goderich in 1827–8. They now suddenly discovered all manner of positive qualities in the leader. David Watt wrote in the *Financial Times* of how Callaghan was proving a 'much more effective Prime Minister than most people had believed possible'. His temper was 'peppery to say the least', but his 'nerve and sense of purpose have been admirable'.[4] Even if his party lagged 15 per cent behind the Conservatives in the polls, a clear majority of the British people expressed their confidence that the Prime Minister was doing a good job. His approval rating far outstripped that of the still uncertain leader of the Opposition, Margaret Thatcher. Whereas Callaghan ran a powerful-looking team, she was still hemmed in by survivors of the old Heath administration—Whitelaw, Carrington, Prior, Pym, Gilmour, and Walker. Also, in a country like Britain (unlike, say, Norway or Iceland), being female did not help her political ratings.

Throughout the spring and summer of 1977, the British economy continued to do astonishingly well. The pound, now a petro-currency, strengthened week by week to reach $1.80 and then $1.90 later in the year; the reserves more than doubled from $4 bn. at the end of December to $7.2 bn. at the end of January and to more than $9 bn. at the end of April.[5] The markets grew stronger and the City more relaxed. More important, the real economy was growing too. Douglas Jay has, quite reasonably, written of the British economic performance between 1977 and 1979 that 'this is one of the few examples of any Western government in the seventies reducing both inflationary pressures and unemployment at the same time'.[6] Denis Healey's budget of March 1977 introduced some relaxation and £2.3 bn. of tax cuts, although the TUC attacked it for linking £1m. of these cuts to a tough pay restraint policy, and for failing to attack unemployment. In effect the citizen was being given back in purchasing power what the Treasury had tried to take away through its massive miscalculation of the Public Sector Borrowing Requirement. However, the markets reacted favourably, and interest rates could safely be cut to 9.5 per cent as gilts hit a four-year peak. Inflation remained in double figures but, with continued pay restraint, could soon be expected to fall. Callaghan told Schmidt it was the darkest hour before the dawn.[7]

Later on, it emerged that the deflation imposed was more severe than was justified because of the quite inaccurate forecasts offered by the Treasury. But the government were victims of convention and civil service misinformation or even disinformation like everyone else at the time. No one had the capacity to offer more authoritative statistics. Still, for the first time for well over a decade, Britain appeared the master of its own economic fate. After the trauma of the IMF negotiations, Healey needed only to draw half the IMF loan offered, and none of the standby credit from central banks after August 1977. The time for freedom from IMF control—what the Chancellor in his Yorkshire vernacular called 'Sod off day'[8]—was coming more rapidly than anyone might have anticipated in the bleak autumn of 1976.

In these distinctly more cheerful circumstances, Callaghan could withdraw from his intense involvement with economic management and leave the conduct of affairs to his Chancellor. But there were areas in which he could take the lead himself, notably in promoting a forward-looking industrial strategy. This had a number of key aspects, both enabling and restrictive. There was the plan for greater industrial democracy through some form of worker participation. There was the continuing need for severe pay restraint on the part of the unions. And there was the wider issue of industrial regeneration to stimulate productive efficiency in the light of the disappointing performance by British industry in 1974–6. Callaghan was personally identified with all these policies, as a goad to the Treasury as much as to both sides of industry. His role, not least as chief communicator, was a highly visible one. His new stance was illustrated by his chairing a meeting of the National Economic Development Council in February and his leading a detailed review of industrial strategy over subsequent weeks.[9]

The first part of the new industrial policy, the move to greater industrial democracy, proved, however, to be abortive. In February 1977 the Committee of Inquiry into Industrial Democracy, chaired by the eminent Oxford historian Alan Bullock, the biographer of Ernest Bevin (and also of Hitler), issued its report. The members of his committee included Jack Jones, general secretary of the Transport Workers, and a strong advocate of worker participation and greater decentralization in industrial management and labour relations, an outlook that reflected his quasi-syndicalist background in Merseyside industry. Others on the committee included David Lea, head of the TUC Economic Department, Clive Jenkins of ASTMS, and the Labour law academic Lord Wedderburn, along with three employers' representatives of whom perhaps the most powerful was Jack Callard, chairman of ICI. The committee was divided, but the majority report clearly favoured an equal number of trade union and shareholders' representatives on the boards of private companies with over 2,000 employees, with a few independents to hold the balance.

Callaghan had gone along strongly with Jack Jones's view of workers' participation on the management board.[10] He was strongly influenced by

Helmut Schmidt's passionate endorsement of German co-determination, deeply rooted in German industrial history over many decades. Callaghan's natural stance was to try to move on from a purely adversarial system of industrial relations to what would in the 1990s be called by 'New Labour' a system of stakeholding with mutual rights and obligations. He arranged and attended a meeting held in Germany between the members of the Bullock Committee and Helmut Schmidt and other key German figures. The German Chancellor argued strongly that Britain's confrontational system, allied to time-worn and inbred patronage methods operated by British management, was fundamentally harmful to the United Kingdom's industrial performance. It was a major reason why the German economy was so much more successful. He poured scorn on the idea that worker directors would harm the flow of private investment, with copious examples from German industrial experience. He attached much hope, as he was to affirm to the present writer eighteen years later, to creating an industrial transformation in Britain which would strengthen its international standing also. Callaghan, as a former trade union official who understood the problems and the psychology of industrial relations at first hand, was the man to achieve it.[11]

The Bullock report was not an extreme document. The Policy Unit correctly pointed out that it argued for a gradual approach. There would be a right to industrial democracy, but no executive order to impose it. The TUC general secretary Len Murray, an enthusiast now both for German co-determination and Swedish social market policies, was a warm supporter.[12] But, like all attempts to reform management–labour relations in British industry, it fell on stony ground. The managers were almost to a man resistant to workers' representatives being elected to their boards of directors. The CBI led a strong outcry against it. It would let loose unpredictable trade unionists into the closed world of the boardroom. The fact that the Bullock proposals would apply only to larger companies where a high degree of union involvement already existed was ignored. Some right-wing journalists, like the newly converted figure of Paul Johnson, a former editor of the *New Statesman*, denounced the influence of the Transport Workers' leader, who was described variously as the most powerful man in Britain and the 'Emperor Jones', echoing a famous American black musical. Amongst the unions, there was resistance across the spectrum to the idea of workers becoming bosses and their historic role thereby being compromised. Jack Jones and David Lea had tended to underestimate the degree of opposition in other unions. Relatively right-wing unions like the Engineers and the General and Municipal Workers joined the miners and the massed forces of the left in denouncing Bullock (a name which was paraphrased in less genteel nomenclature).

Some ministers, notably Edmund Dell, strongly resisted change. Others noted the commercial fiascos that had resulted from recent workers' co-operatives launched by Tony Benn during his time at Trade and Industry, such as Meriden motor cycles, the Fisher-Bendix plant (which, incomprehensibly, produced orange juice as well as car radiators) at Kirby, and the *Scottish Daily News* in Glasgow. They were derided as 'Benn's follies', financial disasters one and all. The Bullock report was offloaded to a Cabinet committee which included both Dell and Shirley Williams, both of them felt to be unsympathetic to its message. Shirley Williams chaired this committee as Paymaster-General. While she hailed the virtues of industrial democracy in her later book *Politics is for People*, she disliked the elements of union power enshrined in Bullock. Her preference was for workers' representatives on boards of directors to be elected directly rather than have the unions claim to represent them. Her committee produced a modest white paper, and it was never heard of again.[13] Industrial relations continued their negative, adversarial pattern. Callaghan's hopes of breaking through the barriers of class and economic power which held back British industrial performance were doomed to disappointment.

Elsewhere, however, the industrial strategy showed some real signs of progress. Despite all pressures and complaints, the policy of pay restraint agreed with the TUC in the summer of 1976, before the IMF crisis broke, held firm for the moment, even though the TUC had voted for a 'planned and orderly' return to free collective bargaining after the summer of 1977. Callaghan and Healey, backed solidly by Foot, urged the vital need for a third year of pay restraint. Callaghan had made a particular point of giving assurances to Jack Jones about a continuing social contract soon after becoming Prime Minister.[14] In return for their moderation, the TUC accepted the government's side of the bargain that the social contract implied, including social benefits and the public ownership of aircraft and shipbuilding. The Advisory and Conciliation Service (ACAS), a central part of the social contract negotiated by Michael Foot when he was at Employment, was already in place. Under the chairmanship of Jim Mortimer, a former trade unionist of left-wing background, it was already achieving a high degree of authority in handling potential labour disputes. There were also attacks on the unemployment problem such as temporary employment subsidies, job creation schemes, and measures to improve industrial training and retraining. Jack Jones later accepted that the TUC in effect obtained everything it could reasonably want in return for pay restraint. As the pound strengthened, the current account steadily improved and the deficit was whittled away. April was an especially good month with the trade surplus being £111m., the strongest performance since October 1971. Crude oil exports were doubled.[15] Britain was manifestly benefiting now from North Sea oil, where BNOC was presiding over the production of 550,000 barrels a day, amounting to close to a third of Britain's needs. By 1980, as Tony Benn affirmed, Britain would be self-sufficient, with production of about 20m. tonnes of oil a year.[16] It would be its own master, free from thraldom to Arab sheikhs in OPEC. The country was also virtually self-sufficient in gas supplies, with 97 per cent of its needs also coming from the beneficent reserves of the North Sea.

If the economic prospects were improving, however, the government's political fortunes were anything but secure. Since the start of Callaghan's period it had been a minority government. By the start of 1977, following adverse by-election results, its original tally of 319 seats (out of a House of 634, excluding the Speaker) had been whittled down to 314. There had been another unexpected loss in early December. Reg Prentice, a former member of Callaghan's Cabinet who had faced violent left-wing opposition in his Newham constituency in London and who had been supported there by Roy Jenkins, Shirley Williams, and others, announced his disillusion with Labour. He would no longer support the government. There followed a fierce public exchange of letters with Callaghan.[17] In due time, as noted above, Prentice was to become a Conservative MP and to serve for a period in Mrs Thatcher's government.

Meanwhile, the government's policy of pay restraint, cuts in public expenditure which added to unemployment, and a monetary policy of cash limits aroused immense anger in Labour ranks, relieved although they may have been that the IMF crisis had not led to Armageddon. Meetings of the Cabinet and the Liaison Committee were invariably tense and bad-tempered affairs. Left-wing Executive members led the attack on the government's reactionary policies as they saw them and called for more socialism. They found a frequent ally in Barbara Castle, a bitter critic who had many fierce clashes with Callaghan himself. In the House, the government had no secure majority at all, and was reduced to bartering for votes with miscellaneous groups of Welsh and Scottish Nationalists and occasional Ulster representatives such as Gerry Fitt of the SDLP. His colleague Frank Maguire, 'Independent Republican' and licensed publican, in effect a supporter of Sinn Féin, was regarded as hostile and in any case seldom turned up at Westminster.

The government now suffered a series of parliamentary defeats on industrial and economic policy. Measures to nationalize the aircraft and shipbuilding industries were making slow progress and facing delay in the House of Lords, which again became a target of Labour attack. There was also trouble on aspects of the Welsh and Scottish Devolution Bill which was now beginning its weary crawl through the Commons under the direction of Michael Foot. On 8 February the government met with defeat on a Reduction of Redundancy Rebates Bill (by a ludicrous mix-up over pairing, Callaghan's own vote for the government was not recorded), and there was a 29-vote defeat over the guillotine on the Devolution Bill on 24 February.[19] The Labour whips, headed by Michael Cocks, did their best: the deputy whip, Walter Harrison, was to become a Westminster legend in these years for his dextrous mixture of persuasion and coercion in getting his flock to support the government in the lobbies.[20] But the Labour ranks were often exhausted beyond normal levels of endurance by long hours and late nights in the House, and unmollified by the pleasures of Annie's Bar, which saw its halcyon period at this time. They were hard to keep under control. Solid trade unionists, especially in the public sector, were discontented by a policy which had seen their members' living standards actually fall for two years running. In fact, the government's record in the lobbies was appalling throughout the Callaghan period. In all, the government was to be defeated on no less than 42 occasions in the five years 1974–9, more than 30 of them under Callaghan's premiership, though never on a formal vote of confidence until the very end. On this basis, the government was simply unable to govern.

A serious personal blow also came at this time. Tony Crosland, the Foreign Secretary, unexpectedly fell ill and died on 19 February. It was an immense personal loss for Callaghan and a tragedy for devoted social democrats for whom Crosland had been philosopher and inspiration for twenty years and more. After some consideration, Callaghan startled the political world by replacing him with his youthful deputy, the 38-year-old David Owen, much the youngest Foreign Secretary since Anthony Eden in 1935. It was a calculated blow on behalf of youth by a premier anxious that his team should not appear stale. Callaghan had long formed a high opinion of Owen as a possible leader in the making, and Owen soon showed his capacity as a strong, if sometimes domineering, minister.[21] He struck up a good relationship with his American counterpart, Cyrus Vance. But Crosland's death manifestly weakened a floundering government still further at a most difficult time. Rock bottom was reached on a threatened adjournment debate on 17 March which Mrs Thatcher promised to regard as a motion of confidence. Callaghan, who had been away on a visit to see President Carter in Washington and had then flown on to Ottawa on 10–13 March, was told at 9 p.m. that evening that the government could not win since all the other groups in the House would be arrayed against it.[22] In the end, ministers had to take the humiliating course of advising Labour members to abstain. The Tory motion was carried by 293 votes to none.

Yet salvation was at hand. Talks with the Scottish Nationalists had been inconclusive, although their commitment to devolution meant that on votes of confidence they were likely to support the government. Plaid Cymru were somewhat firmer, perhaps a reflection of the radical Welsh political ethos, but they numbered only three MPs. Of these three, Dafydd Wigley was in effect a social democrat; Dafydd Elis Thomas was distinctly on the left; Gwynfor Evans, their long-term leader, was a green-minded rural nonconformist pacifist who hated centralization. It was as though a party consisted of Roy Jenkins, Tony Benn, and Jonathon Porritt. This variegated trio were a frail reed on which to rely.

There were some hopes of a liaison with the traditionally conservative Ulster Unionists, a miscellaneous group under the effective leadership of Enoch Powell, one of the wilder cards on the political scene. Powell urged the need for greater Northern Irish representation at Westminster, and had talks with Michael Foot, via Roy Mason the Northern Irish Secretary, about a possible Speaker's Conference on the issue.[23] There was also murmuring on the desirability of an oil pipeline to link Ulster with the British mainland.

However, the intractable problems of Ulster politics made any progress on this front speculative. One stumbling block was the future impact of direct elections to the European Assembly, where the generally pro-Labour SDLP under Gerry Fitt demanded some form of proportional representation, preferably the single transferable vote, to enhance Catholic/Nationalist representation.[24] Callaghan had a private meeting with James Molyneaux and the variegated group of ten who made up Ulster Unionist representation in the Commons at 5.30 p.m. on 16 March (after which he had dinner with the Apostolic Delegate, at Wimbledon).[25] There were further talks with Roy Mason, while Foot and McNally had private discussions with the Unionists about either a Speaker's Conference on Ulster's parliamentary representation or the reform of local government in Northern Ireland. Kenneth Stowe of the prime minister's office was another active go-between. But nothing concrete seemed to emerge. Enoch Powell and James Molyneaux were both prepared to do a deal with Labour. By 1979 Labour had agreed to Enoch Powell's demand for extra seats for Northern Ireland, to the fury of the SDLP. But now the majority of the Unionists, fearful of security considerations as the Provisional Sinn Féin continued a long and accelerating series of bloody atrocities directed upon the civil population, would not budge.[26] Offence was taken at a remark by Mason that Ulster was 'a one-party state'. Kenneth Stowe, Callaghan's private secretary who was much involved in these discussions, urged the Prime Minister that Foot should see Gerry Fitt of the SDLP, an emotional man who became very angry if he felt he was being taken for granted.[27] Northern Ireland, as usual, was irreconcilable. Yet something had to be done immediately since Mrs Thatcher was to move a vote of no confidence in the government on 23 March.

However, the other element in the political complexities was the Liberals. Here there was genuine hope. They numbered thirteen members of parliament and were under the shrewd tactical leadership of David Steel. Still under 40, he had nevertheless been in the House for twelve years. He had only recently succeeded the discredited Jeremy Thorpe as party leader and was ambitious to make a name. The Liberals were anxious to find a way to increase their influence on key aspects of policy; like the government, they had no particular wish for a general election. There had been unofficial overtures to the government (later disavowed) in February by the independent-minded and distinctly bulky Liberal member for Rochdale, Cyril Smith, once a Labour activist himself. There were also important figures in Labour's ranks who had good personal relations with the Liberals. Several of them were Celts, amongst them Cledwyn Hughes, a friend of such leading Liberals as Emlyn Hooson (Montgomeryshire), a fellow graduate of the University College of Wales, Aberystwyth.[28] There were also members of the Cabinet, such as Shirley Williams and Bill Rodgers, friendly with the Liberals. An important letter was written to Callaghan on 17 March by Cledwyn Hughes, conveying David Steel's wish for his party to be consulted 'on broad policy issues and on legislation'. Steel confirmed that he much preferred Callaghan's leadership to a Tory election victory, and he believed that Labour had a chance of winning in late 1978 to 1979. 'As a new Leader and a young man he felt it would be impertinent for him to approach you and he was glad, therefore, to have the opportunity of giving me these views.'[29]

On the late evening of 17 March, after the adjournment motion had been carried by 293 votes (including the Liberals) to none, Callaghan instructed the whips, Michael Foot and Cledwyn Hughes, to establish formal contact with David Steel; they reported to him at 11.30 a.m. on Friday, 18 March, along with Roy Mason, the Northern Irish Secretary.[30] Extensive soundings followed during the weekend. One important episode was a phone call to William Rodgers from Peter Jenkins of the *Guardian*. Rodgers then phoned David Steel and eventually the Prime Minister (unusually), late on Sunday evening. The message that Rodgers conveyed was that there was agreement between Labour and the Liberals on every issue other than the adoption of PR in the European elections. The decisive contact, clearly, would be that between Callaghan and the youthful leader of the Liberals, David Steel. There was indeed a kind of personal link between them. Callaghan had stayed with Mrs Steel's parents during his visit to Sierra Leone in 1946.

The first manœuvres were unpromising. Steel's initial letter to Callaghan setting out the Liberals' terms infuriated the Prime Minister, who flung it angrily on the floor. Tom McCaffrey and Kenneth Stowe, the only others present, retrieved the letter and persuaded the premier to calm down. Thereafter the outlines of a political pact emerged in the course of that afternoon. There was even a suggestion that Steel himself might at some stage become a Cabinet minister.[31] Callaghan saw Steel alone at 6 p.m. on Monday, 21 March (on returning from his regular haircut appointment at Simpson's in the Strand). The meeting was friendly; Callaghan, much the older man, was warm, almost paternal, towards the boyish Liberal leader. This was followed up by meetings with Foot and Steel at 12.30 p.m. and again at 6 p.m. the next day, followed by another meeting of Callaghan with Steel and his deputy John Pardoe at 7.45 p.m. Even though he and Pardoe were hardly blood brothers, Steel announced that he could carry his small force with him, and the famous Lib–Lab pact came into being.[32]

It contained four main proposals. There would be a consultative committee between the two parties to which any major departmental bill would be referred. There would be regular meetings between the Chancellor and the Liberal economic spokesman John Pardoe. On policy there was agreement on direct elections to the European Parliament, with a free vote on the voting system (though the Liberals wanted PR, and were to 'reaffirm their strong conviction' on its behalf), and a commitment to inject momentum into the flagging cause of Welsh and Scottish devolution, with two separate measures to replace the original bill. A Liberal demand that there should be no further nationalization proposals was set on one side. Subject to these conditions, the Liberals would vote to ensure that the government would not fall in the House of Commons, while keeping their options open on matters of detail.[33]

At midday on the 23rd, the day of the motion of confidence, an emergency meeting of the Cabinet was held. Callaghan, according to Benn, was very flushed, Michael Foot white and drawn. For all the tension of the occasion, however, Callaghan appears to have imposed his authority with remarkable effect. Kenneth Stowe later regarded his as 'a virtuoso performance', comparable to his handling of the Cabinet meetings during the IMF talks.[34] The Prime Minister told his colleagues of the pact with the Liberals. There was no alternative since the vote of confidence would otherwise be lost. A general election had been pencilled in for 5 May. Tony Benn was furious in his opposition, not least because he believed he had been fundamentally misled by Michael Foot; their relationship deteriorated substantially from that time on. But the pact was supported by Healey (who said that a deal with 'Nats and nutters' was the only alternative), Shirley Williams, Mulley, Hattersley, Booth (a left-winger influenced by Foot), Mason, Owen, Elwyn-Jones, Rees, Varley, Dell, Morris, Rodgers, Silkin, Ennals, Lever, and Peart. In the end the Cabinet endorsed the pact by 20 to 4 (Shore, Orme, Benn, and, rather surprisingly, Millan, the centrist Scottish Secretary). Benn then had a strong exchange with Callaghan. His signature had appeared on a left-wing letter organized by Eric Heffer, which denounced any deal with the Liberals as a betrayal of socialist principles. Callaghan responded bluntly that, if Benn signed the letter, he would be dismissed. After earnest discussions with Heffer, Foot, and his wife Caroline, Benn then withdrew his signature, and stayed, against his convictions, in the government.[35] In the event, the government survived the vote of confidence with some ease. The motion of no confidence was defeated by 322 votes to 298, with all thirteen Liberals voting for the government, and three Ulster Unionists, including Enoch Powell, abstaining. The Callaghan administration's lease of life was substantially extended.

The Lib–Lab pact was the essential political corollary to the recent economic success. In July, Steel was to confirm that it would be renewed by the Liberals for the whole of the next parliamentary session. In all, it lasted from March 1977 to August 1978 when the Liberals, by now much divided in counsels, decided to bring it to an end. However evocative of smoke-filled rooms the pact had been, it was an event of considerable political significance. It enabled the Labour government to remain in power with a reasonable expectation of life. It could probably call an election at a moment favourable to the government rather than being harried out of office in the wake of a untidy revolt by miscellaneous backbench fragments. In late June Bernard Donoughue analysed on behalf of the Policy Unit the new situation that had opened up. He wrote to the Prime Minister on 23 June, following further by-election setbacks including the loss of Ashfield, a solid Labour seat in the East Midlands, on 29 April with a 20.9 per cent swing to the Conservatives after David Marquand's departure to Brussels. That meant that the government could count on a tally of 323 votes—310 Labour (including Gerry Fitt but excluding the Nationalist Frank Maguire and Reg Prentice) and 13 Liberals. He might reasonably have included the 3 Plaid Cymru members as well. The Opposition at best could manage 310 (including all the SNP but excluding Maguire). That meant the government was virtually assured of surviving until the end of that parliament. There was now a real prospect of having time to wait for the effects of economic recovery, including a fall in prices and higher take-home pay, to show themselves. Public expenditure could be increased, reflation would boost the economy through higher purchasing power, and the fruits of recovery could be redistributed in the inner cities, and amongst the poor and unemployed. The Lib–Lab pact had created a moment of opportunity.[36]

That was not, of course, how everyone saw it. The Conservatives, naturally, denounced it as a cynical fix, devoid of principle, to keep the government lurching on in office though not in power. The Liberals themselves had divided counsels, with a broad spread of ideological opinion in the party and disappointment that they had not been able to impose PR in the European elections. On the Labour left, there was deep anger. Eric Heffer was foremost in circulating letters of protest and leading movements of dissent which continued reverberating until the summer, with (it was believed) the covert sympathy of Ron Hayward, Geoff Bish, and others in Transport House.[37] Tony Benn regarded it as a great betrayal.[38] Nor did all aspects of the pact develop straightforwardly. While most meetings of ministers with their Liberal counterparts were friendly and civilized, the high-decibel encounters of Denis Healey with John Pardoe, two highly combustible characters, reverberated down the corridors of Westminster. Joel Barnett had to sweep up the mess.[39]

But the pact stuck. Much was owed to the good relationship between Callaghan himself and Steel; the latter considered the Prime Minister to be 'first and foremost a patriot'.[40] Apart from personal courtesies, there can be little doubt that the main advantage of the pact lay strongly with the Labour government. Callaghan had given very little away: powers of consultation and co-operation did not amount to a veto. PR on European elections had been set on one side for the moment, although it remained a continuing difficulty: on 7 June Steel urged Callaghan in vain that the government should make a positive recommendation in favour of PR rather than leave it to a free vote.[41] Otherwise, the government's essential industrial and economic strategy could proceed as before. The one exception was the Local Authority Works Bill, the government's 'last piece of doctrinaire legislation' according to *The Economist*,[42] about which Callaghan had no positive feelings anyway. David had given Goliath a lifeline. The big battalions would continue undeterred, their parliamentary flank secured for as long as anyone could foresee.

One delicate issue which could have caused difficulty was allowed to remain dormant. This was the homosexual relationship of the former Liberal leader Jeremy Thorpe with Norman Scott. Harold Wilson had allowed himself to be implicated in what he regarded as a matter of security involving South African 'dirty tricks' against Thorpe; in February or March 1976 he apparently obtained from Barbara Castle, then at Social Security, the file on Scott's employment by Thorpe some fifteen years earlier. There were many rumours in Westminster about the affair (legal action against Thorpe was probable and David Steel and his party profoundly hoped that it would take place after the next general election). But the connection with Harold Wilson (and also Marcia Williams) remained hidden from public gaze, while in any case Callaghan himself had not even the remotest involvement in the curious behaviour of his former leader.[43]

In return the Liberals had gained minor concessions on a European assembly and devolution. Otherwise they had only the seductive whiff of marginal participation of government to console them after sixty-two years of isolation, apart from wartime and briefly in 1931–2. But there was the prospect of some form of extended Lib–Lab collaboration as in the 1906 parliament, albeit with a totally different balance of power, for which scholar-publicists like David Marquand had long called. Indeed, Marquand's massive and distinguished biography of Ramsay MacDonald which appeared in February 1977 was widely taken as an argument for the Progressive alliance on pre-1914 lines to be disinterred—probably correctly since Marquand was to move on to the SDP and the Liberal Democrats before joining Tony Blair's 'progressive' New Labour again in 1994. Politicians like Shirley Williams and William Rodgers who became Liberal Democrats in the later 1980s looked back to the Lib–Lab pact of 1977–8 as a creative and successful period of stable government that provided them with respectable political ancestry. Whether the pact implied the seeds of an SDP in the making, though, is highly debatable. What it did was to renew Old Labour and give it a credibility it had lacked since the election of 1966.

Fortified by the pact and continuing positive news in the financial columns of the newspapers, the government entered upon a cheerful and almost buoyant summer. Callaghan's own prestige at home and abroad rose substantially. His political troubles behind him, he looked and sounded like a statesman. There was only one incidental problem that troubled him. This was a very odd case, when he was attacked for nepotism and patronage in making his son-in-law Peter Jay ambassador to the United States in May 1977. This was, for once, not handled too well by the usually infallible Tom McCaffrey in the press office who let slip remarks to the effect that Sir Peter Ramsbotham, the present man in Washington, was a snobbish, effete fuddy-duddy. The *Evening Standard* ran the ineffable headline, 'Snob Envoy Had to Go'.[44] Callaghan had to intervene directly both to affirm his faith in Ramsbotham's qualities and also to defend McCaffrey's integrity as a public servant. Callaghan had the highest opinion of Peter Jay's abilities. He had previously considered him for a transfer from the world of the media to a political post, either as political adviser at 10 Downing Street, or indeed as a kind of economic adviser in the Washington embassy around the turn of the year. A proposal that he should 'join the team' as economic adviser had been made during the Christmas period, but Jay declined.[45] As has been seen, Callaghan's famous speech to the Labour Party conference on 28 September 1976 contained a key passage written privately by Jay himself.

However, the idea that he should actually become ambassador in Washington came from the new youthful Foreign Secretary David Owen, who was also a good friend and occasional sailing companion. Jay was summoned to the Foreign Office during April and, to his astonishment, offered the new post. Owen pressed Callaghan (who at first turned the idea down), in a handwritten note as early as 17 March when Owen himself had been at the Foreign Office for less than a month. Jay would be 'an impressive new appointment' and the Prime Minister need not be worried by accusations because the new ambassador was married to his daughter Margaret.[46]

Callaghan himself gave it much thought and discussed the proposal with President Carter on 6 May. He was warned against it by the Cabinet Office. In addition to laying himself open to charges of nepotism, there were doubts whether Peter Jay, whose background lay in the individual enterprise of journalism, had the managerial capacity to run a large embassy. But eventually Callaghan went along with the appointment, not least because of the crucial economic aspect of the Anglo-American relationship where Peter Jay's expertise would be invaluable. Jay himself had also to consider the matter, and talked it over with his head at London Weekend Television, John Freeman, a former parliamentary colleague of

Callaghan's and a one-time ambassador to Washington himself. Margaret Jay was not wholly enthusiastic, in part because of the disruption to the children's schooling.[47] But in the end Jay agreed to accept. Owen then announced the appointment to the diplomatic correspondents of the press on 11 May where it had a hostile reception. The charge of nepotism was thrown freely at Callaghan. American journalists came up with jibes such as 'The son-in-law also rises'. There were vicious attacks from some Labour MPs against both Callaghan and Owen, the latter shortly to be devastated by a very serious illness to his young son. But it passed by and in fact Peter Jay was to prove a capable and unusually numerate ambassador with his skill in economic matters supplemented by much political artistry in handling the Washington political and press Mafia.

Callaghan's summer was a cheerful one, the best he had known for many years. It was crowned by a highly successful hosting of a visit from the new US President Jimmy Carter on 5–7 May. This was followed by the Third World Economic Summit chaired by Callaghan and held in 10 Downing Street on 7–9 May with the heads of government of the United States, France, Germany, Italy, Canada, and Japan represented, and then by a meeting of the North Atlantic Council at Lancaster House on 10 May.[48] All these events were highly successful. As will be seen in the next chapter, Callaghan had already taken pains to cultivate the new American President, notably in a visit to Washington in March and in many subsequent communications. His first appearance in Britain was a most congenial occasion. The highlight was a visit by President and Prime Minister to Durham and the north-east. The President, a warm admirer of the poetry of Dylan Thomas (on whose behalf he successfully pressed the cause of a commemorative plaque in Westminster Abbey), had, it was believed, originally wanted to visit south Wales. But this was deemed to be unacceptable, perhaps because of bias shown by a prime minister who held a Welsh seat.

Carter's visit to Newcastle in brilliantly sunny weather proved to be a huge success.[49] He received the freedom of the city: the Mayor told him that, born a Georgian, Carter had become a Geordie. On the way to Newcastle, Callaghan instructed the President in the famous Newcastle United football cry, 'Hawa' the Lads!' and this went down exceptionally well in the vast Geordie gathering. The merry refrain of the 'Blaydon Races' was omnipresent. Callaghan presented him with a volume of autobiography by that fine old representative of the Durham mining community Jack Lawson, a member of Attlee's Cabinet for a time when Callaghan had first entered parliament, and this was evidently read on the flight home. Carter indeed had plenty of varied reading matter for his return journey since Tony Benn, who was unable to meet him, gave him an inscribed pamphlet he himself had written on the seventeenth-century Levellers and their contribution to democracy. He hoped that it might help the President to reach correct conclusions on current events, including on nuclear policy.[50]

The Downing Street summit was an even more effective event for the Prime Minister, the chairman and genial host, with ample photo opportunities. It was said that the French were angry with the press attention for Callaghan and the suggestion that an English-based summit, conducted in the English language, had been more effective than one held on French soil.[51] There was a general feeling that it had been very productive, more so than its predecessors at Rambouillet or Puerto Rico. In particular, Callaghan seized the opportunity himself of pressing the cause, dear to his heart, of international action to promote economic expansion in the west. Each major government committed itself to specific targets for the stimulation of growth and an attack on unemployment, without lapsing into protectionism. There was also a firmer commitment to assist aid levels and loan programmes for the development of the third world.[52] Potential storms, usually arising from the lack of compatibility of Schmidt and Carter over nuclear fuel policy and other issues, had all been happily averted.

After this series of major events, the summer continued to go well. There were no gloomy financial headlines, and no threat to sterling now that the decision over the sterling balances had been resolved. In fact, the attractiveness of sterling now that the economy was improving meant that the balances stayed distinctly higher than had been anticipated that summer and autumn. But this did not cause any international concern.[53] On the political front, discussions with the National Executive continued to be often unpleasant, notably when in late May the report of Reg Underhill, the former national agent, showed clear evidence of Trotskyist 'entryism', notably by Militant Tendency, into local constituency parties. On this occasion Michael Foot led the cry that there should be no witch-hunt, adding that there had always been Marxists in the Labour Party and citing the historic judgement of Clement Attlee to this effect.[54] No action, therefore, was taken against left-wing infiltration. A scourge remained for Callaghan, Foot, and the rest of the leadership in future years. At the parliamentary level, things were now much quieter. The pact with the Liberals was renewed for another year, and the recess was reached in a tranquil mood. The Prime Minister could enjoy a variety of events to celebrate the Queen's silver jubilee as a monarch. One that had a particular emotional poignancy for him was attendance at his native city of Portsmouth on the royal yacht *Britannia* on 27 June to witness the naval review at Spithead. Sixty-five years earlier his father had been a rigger aboard the royal yacht of the day, the *Victoria and Albert*, when King George V had presided.[55] Then the Prime Minister retired to Ringmer for a somewhat fragmented leisure period punctuated by a variety of visits from foreign dignitaries including Dr Kurt Waldheim and Cyrus Vance, the US Secretary of State.

That summer, the economic recovery seemed to go on and on. Sterling continued to rise to over $1.80. Indeed the government was shortly to take action to prevent its rising still further and thereby harming the performance of British exports. The Bank of England sold sterling for dollars in large quantities, but the pound continued to rise to $1.90 and beyond. In November Healey decided to allow it to float for a time, to avoid a possible rise in interest rates. The reserves reached a record level of $14.85 bn. by mid-September with a steady increase in demand for the pound. The very rapid inflow of sterling, indeed, caused some anxiety in the Policy Unit. Bernard Donoughue argued the case for lowering interest rates to slow it down; Gavyn Davies suggested a cap of around $1.75 on the value of the pound. Donoughue pointed out that, despite the government's intended policy of winding up sterling's role as a reserve currency, the sterling balances had actually risen by no less than $2 bn. since the start of the year, and the IMF became more concerned.[56] Shares on the stock exchange reached an unprecedentedly high level on 14 September, with the *FT* 30-share index standing at 592.2. This was 5.6 per cent higher than the previous record in May 1972 at the height of the unstable Barber boom. The balance of payments was steadier than for a decade. It moved from a deficit of £511m. in the third quarter of 1976 to a surplus of £483m. in the third quarter of 1977. August saw the largest ever surplus in one month at £316m.[57] The current account was in surplus for five months running from August to December. In January, it was announced that Britain had had a trade surplus for the year 1977, the first that decade.[58]

These abstract statistics were being translated now into terms that the ordinary citizen could appreciate. As opinion polls showed, what a later generation would call a 'feel-good factor' was at work. Interest on home loans, once in double figures, went down to 8.5 per cent in January. With the assistance of the Price Commission, prices were now manifestly falling, as they had not done for some years. Inflation in January 1978 was in single figures; the RPI showed that at 9.9 per cent it was at its lowest since the price explosion of October 1973 in the days of the Heath government. The Chancellor's autumn budget in October offered also a major reflation of £1 bn. in the current year and £2.2 bn. in the next. Increases in tax allowances and rise in public spending amounted to 'a considerable recovery in real take-home pay and personal consumption' for 1978, according to the *Financial Times*.[59] The Policy Unit, which had been arguing the case for a £3 bn. reflationary package, noted that higher tax allowances would be more advantageous for the poorly paid as well as being popular with higher income groups which had 'suffered a massive reduction in their living standards in the past two years'.[60] The ordinary citizen found himself with higher take-home pay, lower prices, and falling unemployment—an almost unbeatable recipe. Not surprisingly, for the first time the government found the opinion polls at long last beginning to move its way. In December 1977 there was actually a Labour lead of 0.5 per cent recorded, although things began to slip again in the new year. Even so, there were reasonable grounds for believing that the Prime Minister could now consider possible dates for a general election.

The economy at this time was benefiting from more cheerful global circumstances, Britain's recovery being in some measure part of a worldwide economic revival in the major industrial nations. But it was also benefiting from a more flexible course of policy. The economic seminars chaired by the Prime Minister were in full swing that autumn and ranged over a variety of central issues. Callaghan himself noted three excellent meetings on 28 October, 22 November, and 8 December: 'Harold Lever wrote a series of perceptive commentaries on Interest Rates, the Gilt-Edged Market, the decline of the dollar (and the need for a co-operative money system) in which I agreed with him.'[61] Denis Healey believed that these meetings stemmed in part from the Prime Minister's long-developed sense of distrust about the Treasury and its philosophy, but he felt that they nevertheless were helpful in keeping No. 10 and the Treasury in close touch. Callaghan himelf felt they offered a forum to discuss the future of sterling in the longer term beyond the Chancellor's preoccupation with day-to-day management. At the top at any rate, there was harmony in economic management.[62]

At all points the role of the Prime Minister was central. SuperJim seemed to be replacing the legendary SuperMac. Like his Tory predecessor, he was enjoying the job as well as apparently doing it well. He had been the key figure at the start of the summer in negotiating with the TUC Economic Committee for a continuance of pay restraint. This time it was much more difficult than in 1975 or 1976, with Congress having urged the return to free collective bargaining. The TUC Committee as a whole was almost intractable, consisting as it did of a wide variety of members including irreconcilable left-wingers such as Alan Fisher of NUPE. On the other hand, more common sense was likely to come from Len Murray, the pragmatic TUC general secretary, as well as the trade union members of NEDC. They included the two major figures of Jack Jones and Hugh Scanlon, both close to retirement, along with other moderate figures such as Alf Allen of the Shopworkers, David Basnett, and Geoffrey Drain. They persuaded the TUC Committee to issue a remarkably moderate statement on 19 July, which called for the avoidance of a pay explosion and empha- sized the adverse consequences for inflation if pay increases went above 10 per cent. In the circumstances this was quite as much as the government could have hoped for.[63] Meanwhile, possible compromises were being floated. Gavyn Davies of the Policy Unit suggested the indexation of wage claims to meet the acknowledged recent drop in take-home pay. Relating wages to the domestic price index rather than the RPI would, he argued, be much safer and less potentially inflationary. It would be less affected by the global economy.[64] At the 1977 TUC annual congress at Blackpool at the start of September the Economic Committee's pronouncement of 19 July in favour of a renewal of the 'twelve-month rule' on pay claims was endorsed by nearly 3 million votes. Even though free collective bargaining was also reaffirmed, an essential component of the fight against inflation and on behalf of economic recovery had been achieved once again.

There was much debate amongst advisers at this point as to what eco- nomic and, ultimately, political conclusions the Prime Minister should draw. In general, the Think Tank tended to be cautious, even pessimistic, the Policy Unit, with its sharper political antennae, more optimistic. On 17 June 1977, Gavyn Davies was able to point to several positive aspects of the development of the economy which left room for much net fiscal reflation over coming months and years. He outlined the prospect of successive reflationary budgets with income tax basic rate being reduced to even 15 per cent by 1982, a heady scenario indeed.[65] Bernard Donoughue outlined the case for successive boostings of public spending and cuts in interest rate. It was generally agreed that the general election should be deferred for at least a year. But some time in late 1978 or early 1979 there would be a 'window' when unemployment was falling, the balance of payments was in surplus, inflation was steady, and take-home pay was rising.[66]

Callaghan himself hammered these points home in a series of major addresses to Labour audiences that summer. At an all-Wales rally in Aberystwyth, he went on to outline the more fundamental values for which a social democratic party and movement should strive—democracy (political and industrial), control of size, production for need not for profit, community care for all, neighbourliness, and a new basis for international relations.[67] Throughout that autumn and winter he struck an increasingly confident note. In an interview with Gordon Clough on BBC radio's *The World this Weekend* he described the components of the economic recovery that had continued throughout 1977. It was, he declared confidently, 'the year in which the pendulum has swung our way'.[68]

One fundamental aspect of the growing economic prosperity the Prime Minister somewhat skated over. This was the growing revenue coming in from North Sea oil. This was a massive potential benefit which could add £3–4 bn. to GNP in 1980 and up to £5 bn. in 1985, a huge source of revenue and a vast saving in foreign currency. A major, if predictable, difference of view on this emerged in Cabinet. Denis Healey urged that the oil revenues be used for long-term investment and paying off liabilities; Tony Benn argued the case for national development on behalf of social priorities. A meeting on 9 November 1977, attended by Healey and Derek Scott for the Treasury, and Benn and Frances Morrell for the Energy Department, produced total deadlock. Healey wanted the oil revenue used for tax cuts and debt repayment, Benn wanted to rebuild the manufacturing base. Callaghan decided to handle this in a remarkably Rooseveltian way, by trying to 'weave the two together'. Here was the Prime Minister in presidential mode, as supreme mediator, as FDR had been over tariffs or public works in 1933. Callaghan now asked Healey and Benn to produce a joint paper on the likely extent of the oil revenues and their possible beneficial uses. In strictly impartial terms, he also minuted Tom McNally, 'Please tell Mr. Healey and Mr. Benn that they are both trying to do too much too soon.' Bernard Donoughue, meanwhile, was trying to propose a compromise, not least because of a fear that Benn might otherwise go public and make known his own 'socialist' views.

All this was not without its entertaining aspects, but the outcome was fortunate from Callaghan's point of view. A joint paper signed by Healey and Benn and presented to the Liaison Committee on 21 November merely listed the possible options—overseas investment, foreign debt repayment, and tax reductions on Healey's side, the public services and social infrastructure, investment in manfacturing industry and energy resources on Benn's. It may be suspected that a majority of Labour supporters, many of them far from being on the left, would have taken Benn's side in this dialogue. But, given the balance of power in the Callaghan administration, there could only be one winner. On 16 February 1978, the Cabinet took the view, by a large majority which included Michael Foot, that oil revenue should be absorbed into general revenue and used for general Treasury purposes, which might include capital investment, debt redemption, or perhaps tax cuts.[69] Economics ministers like Harold Lever and Joel Barnett shredded Benn's proposals, for which there was much support in the party in the country. It was another defeat for the Tony Benn 'alternative strategy', a further victory for the Callaghan brand of centrism, as opposed to more interventionist forms of socialism.

In the first part of 1978 the good news continued, although less consistently than in 1977. The focal point of Healey's April budget was a programme of £2 bn. in tax cuts to regenerate a growth of 3 per cent in the economy. This went through although only narrowly. A sum of £1 bn. was repaid to the IMF; Britain had already agreed not to draw on its full entitlement of credits. On 16 June, in one of the last manifestations of the Lib–Lab pact, the Liberals supported the government in their 287 : 282 victory, by backing a package which included a 2.5 per cent surcharge on employers' national insurance contributions to finance a cut in the standard rate of income tax.[70] On the other hand, to counter possible overheating, the minimum lending rate was increased to 7 per cent. On 5 May it went up to 8.75 per cent after strong international pressure on interest rates. There was a deficit on the current account of £170m. in March. But it was followed by a large surplus of £336m. in April,[71] and further surpluses in May and June. The fall in prices was now very evident to the ordinary consumer. Callaghan told the Commons on 6 June that a level of 7 to 8 per cent inflation should be sustained for some time before falling again. There were many signs of a growth in consumer spending and much buoyancy in house purchase, that popular icon of private affluence, cheap credit, and upward mobility, despite rises in interest rates. Old Labour Britain had never had it so good.

Most of the political cards now seemed in the government's hands. They had had a long fifteen-month run of remarkably good news, free from the banana skins that seemed so regularly to disturb the various Harold Wilson governments. The government seemed competent, honest, and scandal-free. No spy stories or slag mountains now to dent its prestige. The opinion polls, though volatile, offered much better reading with Tories and Labour within range of each other. In a potentially tricky by-election in Scotland on 2 June, in Hamilton, the scene of a famous Scottish Nationalist victory back in 1967, the Labour candidate easily defeated the SNP representative.

The Prime Minister himself regularly scored well in pollings of the voters, easily surpassing Mrs Thatcher every time. His television and radio interviews struck the right balance between prudence and optimism. Cledwyn Hughes noted the Prime Minister's high reputation in all quarters. On 23 February 1978 Denis Healey was conveying 'high praise of Jim Callaghan with whom he gets on well'.[72] On 2 March he was having a friendly lunch with Tony Benn, with whom he had an ancestral bond in view of their common nonconformist background, and for whose father he had a strong regard. 'He praised Jim Callaghan, comparing him favourably with Harold Wilson. Everyone is praising Jim. I hope it does not go to his head.'[73] Others on the Labour side entertained the same hopes and fears after it was reported (in fact, totally misreported) that Peter Jay, the new ambassador in Washington, had compared his father-in-law the Prime Minister to none less than Moses. Mrs Thatcher, in a laboured joke provided for her by Sir Ronald Millar, responded in her speech to the Conservative Party Conference by urging Moses to 'keep taking the tablets'. (According to Alan Watkins, she herself would have preferred the more entertaining, though perhaps more *risqué*, joke, 'Keep taking the pill'.[74])

In fact, the Moses story was misunderstood and actually makes the reverse point. Callaghan was the last person to allow economic good news and political omens to go to his head. In conversation with Peter Jay in a walk along the South downs at Firle Beacon, the Prime Minister had indeed compared himself to Moses, but as a leader who set changes in train but might yet fail to see the promised land.[75] He well knew that the prospects for the longer term were still uncertain. On the surface, it might have seemed in the cheerful summer of 1978 as though things were moving his way, economically and politically, and that it was simply a matter of choosing the most suitable time for the next election for the reward to be his. In fact, there were many difficulties. The experience of being the head of a minority government was a constant strain, despite the bolstering effect of the Lib–Lab pact. Parliamentary embarrassments continued. As late as May 1978 there were two defeats on the committee stage of the Finance Bill. In the first, on 9 May, the government failed to carry its provisions on income tax, when the Ulster Unionists voted with the Conservatives to cut the basic rate of income tax by 1 per cent. On 11 May it was the Scottish Nationalists in this variegated Commons who joined in defeating the government over the level of higher tax rates being raised to £8,000.[76]

One difficulty here was the renewed tension that developed between the Prime Minister and his old Cardiff comrade, the Speaker, George Thomas. There were many points of friction between the two. This was reflected in 1985 in Thomas's memoirs (when he had become Lord Tonypandy) in which harsh observations are made about Callaghan, Foot, and Cledwyn Hughes amongst others, and some constitutionally improper revelations made about confidential discussions behind the Speaker's chair. The tension between Speaker and government ministers had begun early on, in 1976. Thomas had declared the government's Aircraft and Shipbuilding Bill to be a hybrid measure which thus required special parliamentary procedure. The Speaker believed that Callaghan 'never forgave him' after that.[77] Callaghan later took fierce issue with the Speaker's decision on Standing Order 9 (in relationship to British Leyland) on 1 March and called out loudly 'Bad! Bad!' He wrote privately, 'Not even our friendship can prevent me from saying that your S.O.9 decision was bad and should never have been given.' In effect, Callaghan had been compelled, so he felt, to make a statement before he had had enough time to consider the matter. 'I've often heard Speakers recognise that Govts. have rights too—not to be hurried when important issues are at stake—for which they carry the responsibility not the House.'[78] In November 1977 Callaghan complained that while it had been agreed that the Prime Minister should answer in the House questions which 'raise wider and important issues', indirect questions to him had increased and multiplied.[79] There was some sign of coolness between the clerk of the house and the government whips.[80] Relations were later patched up somewhat, but many ministers felt that 'Brother George' in the Speaker's chair had become another cross they had to bear.

The Prime Minister, however, had political troubles of a more basic kind. Despite sniping from left-wingers on the National Executive, the party conference of 1977 was a more serene affair with the government's economic policy given a somewhat grudging endorsement, pay restraint and all. Barbara Castle, somewhat unexpectedly, made a helpful and conciliatory speech. The Prime Minister was in relative control. Tony Benn noted that, while his speech contained 'the old economic nonsense', he got a standing ovation.[81] It was perhaps the last occasion in Labour Party history when the old trade union barons were still comfortably in charge of the conference and supportive of the leadership. A particular influence at this time was David Basnett of the Municipal Workers. He told Tony Benn on 28 September of his long friendship with Callaghan, whom he described (wrongly) as Labour's first working-class leader. Benn responded in similar vein: 'I get on with him extremely well. I much prefer him to Harold.'[82] Among other things, this conversation suggests that it would have been unwise for the Prime Minister to give the impression of taking the proud and hypersensitive David Basnett too casually.

But these genial sentiments could not conceal the growing rift through-out this period between grass-roots hard-left constituency activists and a moderate leadership. The decision not to open the Pandora's box of the Underhill report on 'entryism' was a sign of the potential conflict that lay within. Callaghan had ample experience of it in his own Cardiff con-stituency where Militant or other Trotskyist spokesmen such as Andrew Price and Terry Burns continued their attacks on him, which all Jack Brooks's watchfulness was needed to repel. The importance of left-wing MPs critical of the goverment was likely to be more damaging now that the Liberals, after much heart-searching, had decided to end the eighteen-month pact at the end of the summer of 1978. John Pardoe and others of their members had never been enthusiastic. The final straw was the failure to have proportional representation made the basis of the European Assembly elections in 1979. On the other hand, Callaghan had continued to confide in Steel and to treat the younger man with kindness and appar-ent consideration. They had, for instance, held discussions on possible election dates, which Steel believed would result in an autumn general election in 1978.[83]

There was even more potential trouble from the unions. Grass-roots protests against pay restraint, voiced by shop stewards in the car industry and by public sector workers, were growing. The prospect of firm leader-ship to hold them in check was doubtful with the simultaneous retirement of the two giants of the left, Jack Jones and Hugh Scanlon. The succession to Jack Jones of Moss Evans, a wordy Welshman who resisted attempts for the Transport Workers' executive to impose central control on branch activists, was worrying to the Labour leaders. Still, on the whole, the TUC guidelines and moderation prevailed during the winter and there were no damaging strikes.

One alarming exception was a strike by the Union of Fire Brigades which had put in a claim for a pay rise of 30 per cent and a forty-two-hour working week. Callaghan took charge of events personally. He had a tense meeting with Terry Parry, the general secretary, and the rest of his union executive, on 29 November. Here he pointed out the need to fight infla-tion; a settlement for the firemen could not be isolated from pay rises and comparability formulae for other workers. He urged that the firemen negotiate with the local authorities on the old formula with 'a specially guaranteed position' for the FBU.[84] The discussion ended with Callaghan's blank observation, 'Your strike will not win. You cannot be allowed to succeed.' Peter Rockley, an FBU executive member, commented on this episode, 'He certainly was the most determined person I had ever met.' The Prime Minister declared, according to Rockley, 'I stand or fall [*sic*] that no one will beat the 10 per cent this year.' As they left, one delegate noted the design of the letters 'J.C.' on the stripe of his suit (in fact a gift from a Yorkshire manufacturer, Moxon's). Did the letters mean 'James Callaghan'? No, responded a Derbyshire delegate, 'Jesus Christ'.[85] The firemen's strike went on until the end of January. The government, with memories of the Heath government in mind, refrained from having a state of emergency but sought to break the strike by the use of 20,000 troops as firemen and the use of 'green goddess' emergency fire engines.[86] In the end the firemen went back to work at the end of January with the forty-two-hour week achieved but not the pay increase they had demanded. On a snowy day in Bridlington, Terry Parry faced firemen chanting 'no surrender' who then punched and injured him.[87] But, thanks in large measure to the Prime Minister personally, the government's thin red line on pay restraint had just about held.

Throughout this period, the Callaghan government, which rested on maintaining a close relationship with the unions, faced the dilemma that these unions were increasingly an object of unpopularity and even fear. The great strikes (many unofficial) and almost uncontrolled pay claims of the period from 1970 to 1975 had seeped into the popular consciousness, despite the efforts of Jack Jones and others to achieve restraint thereafter. Strikes seemed more aggressive and socially irresponsible. The ability of hitherto little-regarded groups of workers, such as the water workers for instance, to use industrial muscle to promote their economic objectives caused much anxiety. Secondary picketing in particular had appeared as a new terror since Arthur Scargill's flying pickets in 1972. The public mood changed as a result.

One defining event of this period was the Grunwick strike in the summer of 1977. This arose in the Grunwick Film Processing Laboratories in north London, when an Anglo-Indian entrepreneur, George Ward, refused to allow his largely Asian and female workforce to join the white-collar union APEX. A mass picket developed with strong TUC support. The unions involved in the Grunwick dispute had the most powerful of cases. What Ward was doing was inequitable if not openly illegal. The workforce were only claiming standard rights of union membership and representation. The unions and union leaders involved, Roy Grantham of APEX and Tom Jackson of the Postal Workers, were impeccably moderate. The three government ministers who joined pickets outside the Grunwick works, Shirley Williams, Fred Mulley, and Denis Howell, were regarded as being on Labour's right wing. Yet in the end what lodged in the popular consciousness was not the legal niceties or considerations of social or moral justice, but the extreme violence with which the mass picketing of Grunwick was attended. There were attacks on Grunwick vehicles and on the police. Trotskyist and other left-wing groups not related to the Grunwick company in any way joined in mob action. A young policeman, lying in the road in a pool of blood, made bad news in the press. George Ward's brand of industrial tyranny escaped unscathed. Grunwick became not a fight for workers' rights but a symbol of mob rule and the uncontrolled threat from trade union power.

Similarly, the public took notice when Sam Silkin, the Attorney-General, declined to take any action when the Union of Postal Workers illegally refused in a week of action to handle mail for South Africa. The unions seemed above the law and to be treated as such by the government's law officer. They, like employers, governments, and monarchs in the past, had apparently ignored Sir Edward Coke's famous dictum in the reign of James I, 'Be you ever so great, the law is above you.' Silkin himself in the case of *Gouriet* v. *Union of Post Office Workers* was strongly criticized to this effect from the bench by the Lord Chief Justice, Lord Denning.

The Callaghan government, therefore, entered a crucial period in the summer of 1978. It faced potential trouble from the unions, from their residual supra-legal power and more immediately their pressure to end curbs on pay. For his part, the Prime Minister insisted that a fourth year of pay restraint, modified in specific directions but overall conforming to a fixed norm, was essential. In private conversations with officials in early 1978 he was talking in terms of a 5 per cent pay norm for 1978–9, half of that agreed with the TUC in July 1977. Healey believed that something more flexible, such as a 'single figure' norm which with wage drift would have meant around 10 per cent, was greatly preferable. Hardly anyone believed that the TUC would accept it. Len Murray believed it was all the result of the Prime Minister's giving in to his 'pretensions to intellectualism' rather than relying on his gut instinct about the unions as he had done in the past.[88] Yet in the summer of 1978 it seemed as if the Prime Minister was about to make a public declaration and to make a further stringent limitation of wage increases a pivot of his policy. It seemed a high-risk strategy.

On the other hand, his position was now a relatively strong one. He was the master of a successful Cabinet which had presided over a lengthy period of economic success. The political prospects were looking much more hopeful, and the Tories were still uncertain. Mrs Thatcher was making little impact so far as Opposition leader. In a potentially difficult debate on pay policy on 25 July, Callaghan tore into her on a variety of issues, including her views on an incomes policy, devolution, and immigration, which he claimed were the product of racial prejudice. Mrs Thatcher's reply, according to the *Financial Times* whose reporter was sympathetic to Callaghan, was 'nervous and faltering'. No Iron Maiden here.[89] Later on he was to launch a pre-emptive strike on the young Winston Churchill when he ventured to raise the issue of the coal industry. The Prime Minister countered with an aggressive and carefully considered attack on his grandfather's sending in the troops to Tonypandy. He condemned the Churchills' 'family vendetta against the miners'.[90] Historians queued up to intervene in *The Times* correspondence columns, most of them supportive of Callaghan's view. As a personality, he commanded the House and, many believed, commanded the country. There was another important dimension. Since April 1976 he had added substantially to his reputation by his apparent statesmanship in international affairs, foreign and colonial, as no prime minister had done since Macmillan's heyday. At home and abroad, his stature had grown. As he returned to Cardiff in warm sunshine in early August, to enjoy the 'blue riband' choral competition at the national eisteddfod, held that year in Sophia Gardens, he might feel that the electoral prize, too, was there for the winning.

1. e.g. Ivor Crewe and Anthony King, *SDP: The Birth, Life and Death of the Social Democratic Party* (Oxford, 1995), ch. 1.

2. *The Times*, 31 Dec. 1976.

3. *Financial Times*, 29 Jan. 1977.

4. Ibid., 10 Jan. 1977.

5. Ibid. 1 Apr. 1977; Kingsley Jones to Nigel Wicks, 8 Feb. 1977 (Callaghan Papers, box 9).

6. Douglas Jay, *Sterling: A Plea for Moderation* (London, 1985), 162.

7. Telephone conversation between Callaghan and Schmidt, 16 Mar. 1977, T59A/77 (Callaghan Papers, box 33).

8. Healey, *The Time of my Life*, 433.

9. *Financial Times*, 13 Jan. 1977.

10. Jones, *Union Man*, 314; interview with Jack Jones.

11. Jones, *Union Man*, 314; interview with Helmut Schmidt.

12. Donoughue memo, 'Meeting with Lord Bullock' (PU 223), 26 Oct. 1976; Donoughue memo, 'Industrial Democracy' (PU 243), 21 Dec. 1976 (private papers). Interview with Lord Murray of Epping Forest.

13. Jones, *Union Man*, 314–15; information from Lord Bullock and Lady Williams; cf. Shirley Williams, *Politics is for People* (London, 1981), 126 ff., where she draws a distinction between a consultative form of workers' representation in industrial management and the statutory form advocated by Bullock.

14. Interviews with Jack Jones and Lord Callaghan.

15. *Financial Times*, 14 May 1977.

16. Kingsley Jones to Nigel Wicks, 8 Feb. 1977 (Callaghan Papers, box 9).

17. Prentice to Callaghan, Callaghan to Prentice, 16 Dec. 1976 (ibid., uncatalogued).

18. Material in Callaghan Papers, box 9.

19. *Financial Times*, 9, 24 Feb. 1977.

20. *Observer*, 28 Jan. 1996.

21. Interview with Lord Callaghan; and Owen, *Time to Declare*, 256.

22. McNally memo on Mar. 1977 political crisis, ? Apr. 1977 (Callaghan Papers, box 10); Prime Minister's diary, 1977 (ibid., box 35).

23. McNally memo (ibid., box 19).

24. Roy Mason to Callaghan, 23 Mar. 1977 (ibid.).

25. McNally to Callaghan, 23 Mar. 1977 (ibid.); Prime Minister's diary (ibid., box 35).

26. McNally to Callaghan, 23 Mar. 1977 (ibid., box 10).

27. Kenneth Stowe to Callaghan, 18 Mar. 1977 (two letters, ibid., box 19).

28. Information from Lord Cledwyn of Penrhos.

29. Cledwyn Hughes to Callaghan, 17 Mar. 1977 (Callaghan Papers, box 19).

30. McNally memo and Prime Minister's diary, 1977 (ibid., box 35).

31. David Steel, *Against Goliath* (London, 1989), 166–7; Lord Callaghan has confirmed this to me.

32. Prime Minister's diary, 1977 (Callaghan Papers, box 35); *The Times*, 24 Mar. 1977.

33. Text in Callaghan, *Time and Chance*, 456–7.

34. Benn, *Conflicts of Interest*, 86 (23 Mar. 1977); interview with Sir Kenneth Stowe.

35. Benn, *Conflicts of Interest*, 85–95 (23–5 Mar. 1977).

36. Donoughue memo, 'The Government's Strategy' (PU 289), 23 June 1977 (Callaghan Papers, box 9).

37. McNally to Callaghan, 23 Mar. 1977 (ibid., box 10).

38. Benn, *Conflicts of Interest*, 87 (23 Mar. 1977).

39. Healey, *The Time of my Life*, 403, refers (presumably metaphorically) to picking up broken crockery.

40. Steel, *Against Goliath*, 167.

41. Stowe to Hunt, 8 June 1977 (private papers).

42. *The Economist*, 26 Mar. 1977.

43 MS memo by ? on 'The Jeremy Thorpe/Norman Scott Affair', 19 Oct. 1977 (private papers).

44. Interviews with Sir Thomas McCaffrey and Peter Jay; Owen, *Time to Declare*, 322.

45. Peter Jay to Callaghan [addressed 'Dear Grandad'], 10 Jan. 1977 (Callaghan Papers, uncatalogued); interview with Peter Jay.

46. Owen to Callaghan, 17 Mar. 1977 (Callaghan Papers, uncatalogued).

47. Interview with Peter Jay.

48. Prime Minister's diary, 1977 (Callaghan Papers, box 35).

49. *The Times*, 8 May 1977.

50. Callaghan, *Time and Chance*, 482; Benn, *Conflicts of Interest*, 128 (9 May 1977). Jack Lawson's autobiography, *A Man's Life* (London, 1944), was one Callaghan had read around the time of his election to parliament. For Benn's views on the Levellers, see Tony Benn, *Arguments for Socialism*, ed. Chris Mullins (London, 1980), 29–33. He

regularly took part in the annual demonstration each May in Burford, Oxfordshire, to celebrate the Levellers besieged in Burford Church by Cromwell's troops.

51. Benn, *Conflicts of Interest*, 130 (9 May 1977), citing David Owen.

52. Material in Callaghan Papers (uncatalogued) and *Time and Chance*, 484–5.

53. Burk and Cairncross, *'Goodbye Great Britain'*, 125–6.

54. Benn, *Conflicts of Interest*, 150–1 (25 May 1977).

55. Callaghan, *Time and Chance*, 461.

56. Memos by Donoughue, 1 July 1977 and 14 Sept. 1977 (PU 285 and 304); memo by Davies, 27 July 1977 (PU 296) (Callaghan Papers, box 9).

57. *Financial Times*, 15 Sept. 1977; *The Economist*, 17 Sept. 1977.

58. Ibid. 17 Jan. 1978.

59. *Financial Times*, 27 Oct. 1977.

60. Donoughue memo for the Prime Minister (PU 306), 26 Sept. 1977 (Callaghan Papers, box 9).

61. Material in Callaghan Papers (uncatalogued).

62. Healey, *The Time of my Life*, 450.

63. *The Times*, 20 July 1977; obituary of Geoffrey Drain, *Guardian*, 7 Apr. 1993.

64. Gavyn Davies to Stowe, 'Pay Policy—an Alternative' (PU 274), 20 May 1977 (private papers).

65. Memo by Gavyn Davies, 'The Medium Term Assessment' (PU 284), 17 June 1977 (Callaghan Papers, box 9).

66. Donoughue memos, 23 June, 6 July 1977 (PU 289) (Callaghan Papers, box 9).

67. Speech text in Callaghan Papers; *The Times*, 4 July 1977.

68. Text of interview in Callaghan Papers, box 12.

69. Benn, *Conflicts of Interest*, 280–1 (16 Feb. 1978).

70. The Liberals were 'incensed' on this point, as is mentioned in Kenneth Stowe to Callaghan, 13 June 1978 (Callaghan Papers, uncatalogued).

71. *Financial Times*, 16 May 1978.

72. Cledwyn Hughes diary, 23 Feb. 1978.

73. Ibid. 2 Mar. 1978.

74. Alan Watkins, *A Conservative Coup* (London, 2nd edn., 1992), 36.

75. Interview with Peter Jay. See letters by Michael Cockerill and Peter Jay in *Spectator*, 9 and 16 May 1992.

76. *The Times*, 10, 12 May 1978.

77. Thomas, *Mr Speaker*, 149.

78. Callaghan to George Thomas, 1 and 8 Mar. 1977 (Lord Tonypandy Papers, National Library of Wales, Aberystwyth, file 126).

79. Draft ruling for Mr Speaker, 1 Nov. 1977 (Tonypandy Papers, file 130).

80. R. D. Barlas to the Speaker, 25 Oct. 1977 (ibid.).

81. Benn, *Conflicts of Interest*, 225 (4 Oct. 1977).

82. Ibid. 219 (28 Sept. 1977).

83. Steel, *Against Goliath*, 175.

84. Record of meeting with executive of Fire Brigades Union, 29 Nov. 1977 (Callaghan Papers, box 9).

85. Victor Bailey (ed.), *Forged in Fire: The History of the Fire Brigades Union* (London, 1992), 253, 420.

86. Keith Jeffery and Peter Hennessy, *States of Emergency* (London, 1983), 241–2.

87. Bailey, *Forged in Fire*, 422. The battered Parry commented afterwards, 'Just think what they would have done to the employers!'

88. Interviews with Lord Healey and Lord Murray of Epping Forest.

89. *Parl. Deb.*, 5th ser., vol. 954, 1379–93 (25 July 1978); *Financial Times*, 26 July 1978. In the vote, the Opposition amendment was lost by 304 to 287, but the motion endorsing government policy was carried by a reduced majority of 296 to 281, with a few Labour left-wingers such as Dennis Skinner, Arthur Lewis, and Arthur Latham abstaining. The Scottish Nationalists and Ulster Unionists voted with the Conservatives; Plaid Cymru abstained; the Liberals and Gerry Fitt of the SDLP voted with the government even though the speech of John Pardoe for the Liberals was generally critical of government policy.

90. On 30 Nov. 1978.